Seattle
CURIOSITIES

Also by Steve Pomper

Is There a Problem, Officer? A Cop's Inside Scoop on Avoiding Traffic Tickets

Curiosities Series

Seattle CURIOSITIES

Quirky characters,
roadside oddities &
other offbeat stuff

Steve Pomper

Guilford, Connecticut

The prices, rates, and hours listed in this guidebook were confirmed at press time. We recommend, however, that you call establishments to obtain current information before traveling.

Copyright © 2009 by Morris Book Publishing, LLC

Photos by the author unless otherwise noted
Map by Daniel Lloyd, copyright © Morris Book Publishing, LLC
Text design: Bret Kerr
Layout artist: Kim Burdick
Project editor: John Burbidge

Library of Congress Cataloging-in-Publication Data
Pomper, Steve.
  Seattle curiosities : quirky characters, roadside oddities & other offbeat stuff / Steve Pomper.
      p. cm.
  Includes index.
  ISBN 978-0-7627-4840-2
  1. Seattle (Wash.)—Description and travel. 2. Curiosities and wonders—Washington (State)—Seattle. 3. Seattle (Wash.)—Miscellanea. 4. Seattle (Wash.)—Guidebooks. I. Title.
  F899.S44P66 2009
  917.97'7720444—dc22
                                                    2009018287

Printed in the United States of America

10 9 8 7 6 5 4 3 2 1

For Jody, Bryan, Heather, and Bobby

contents

★ ★

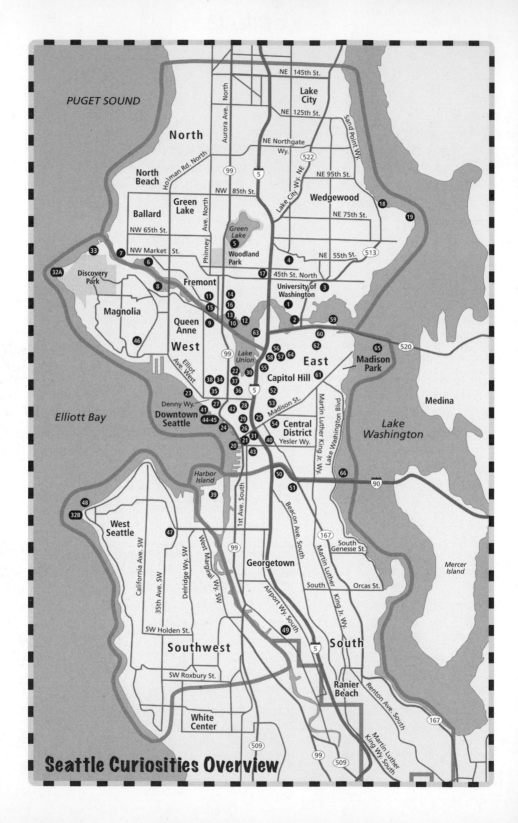

Seattle Curiosities Overview

Map Key

1	University of Washington	33	Fort Lawton
2	Montlake Cut and Bridge	34	Seattle Center
3	Center for Urban Horticulture	35	Space Needle
4	Jet City Improv	36	Monorail
5	Aqua Theater	37	Denny Park
6	Bergen Place Park	38	Experience Music Project (EMP)
7	Ballard Locks	39	Harbor Island
8	Fisherman's Terminal	40	Wing Luke Asian Museum
9	Fremont Bridge	41	Big Picture
10	Aurora Bridge	42	Nordstrom's
11	*The Fremont Rocket*	43	Seattle Underground
12	Gas Works Park	44	Seattle Symphony
13	*Waiting for the Interurban*	45	Hammering Man
14	*The Fremont Troll*	46	Kerry Park
15	Statue of Lenin	47	Luna Park Café
16	Theo's Chocolate Factory	48	Statue of Liberty
17	Hawai'i General Store	49	Museum of Flight
18	*Sound Garden*	50	Taejon Park
19	Sand Point Naval Air Station	51	Northwest African American Museum
20	Ye Olde Curiosity Shop	52	Seattle Museum of the Mysteries
21	The Sinking Ship Garage	53	Cal Anderson Park
22	Center for Wooden Boats	54	Seattle University
23	Olympic Sculpture Park	55	I-5 Colonnade Park
24	Seattle Aquarium	56	G.A.R. Cemetery
25	Freeway Park	57	Confederate Memorial
26	Smith Tower	58	St. Mark's Cathedral
27	Pike Place Public Market	59	Foster and Marsh Islands
28	The Moore Theater	60	Ghost Ramps
29	Bank of America Tower	61	Japanese Garden
30	REI	62	Wilcox Bridge
31	St. James Cathedral	63	Lake Union
32A	Lighthouse (Magnolia)	64	Bruce Lee's Gravesite
32B	Lighthouse (West Seattle)	65	Evergreen Point Floating Bridge
		66	I-90 Floating Bridge

acknowledgments

★ ★

I'd like to thank the folks at Globe Pequot Press for their confidence in me, in particular my editors, for their assistance and good nature. I'm also in debt to the authors of the fine books, e-books, and Web articles, especially those at historylink.org, who've provided me with such valuable resources. And of course a big thanks to my friends and family for all of their tolerance of my pretending to be a temperamental artist, mostly just to get their sympathy and my way.

introduction

★ ★

I really couldn't write a book about Seattle curiosities without beginning with the original Seattle curiosity: the word *Seattle* itself. Seattle is actually a mispronunciation of Chief Sealth (also Seathl or See-ahth), the nineteenth-century Suquamish and Duwamish tribal leader. Friendly to the non-Indian settlers of early Seattle, Chief Sealth developed a friendly relationship with Seattle pioneer David Swinson "Doc" Maynard, who suggested the city be named for the Indian leader; but more on that later. At any rate, before Seattle was called Seattle, the settlement was known as Duwamps. I don't know about you, but the Duwamps Seahawks doesn't really sing for me.

Though not a Seattleite by birth, I am a Seattleite by choice. After bouncing back and forth between New England and Seattle during the early 1980s, my wife, Jody, and I had a decision to make. It was 1986, time to send the oldest of our three children to school. Being tugged by the two coasts, we had to choose where to rear and educate our kids.

My wife preferred that we remain in New England, while I wanted to move to Seattle. So, in an act of compromise that has signified the secret to our now three-decade-long marriage, we decided to remain in New England. As much as I'd fallen in love with Seattle, I'd resigned myself to raise our kids in New England and hoped perhaps someday we could retire to Seattle.

However, to my surprise, Jody changed our mind. Practical as always, she decided that the financial opportunities looked better for our family in Seattle. We still love New England, but Seattle was where we'd build our future. Jody became a firefighter, and I began a law enforcement career. I got serious about my writing around 2003 and became an author in May 2007 with the publication of my book *Is There a Problem, Officer? A Cop's Inside Scoop on Avoiding Traffic Tickets* (The Lyons Press).

What's in a Name?

"S-E-A-T-T-L-E." The word *Seattle* is a smooth, rhythmic word that now graces a world-class American city. But where did the Emerald City get its name? Chief Sealth, a man in his sixties, was leader of the Duwamish and Suquamish tribes who lived in this area at the time non-Indian settlers arrived.

Seattle is a mispronunciation of the great Chief 's name, originally pronounced *Sealth* (as in *Health)* or *See-alth.* How the mispronunciation came into common usage is open to speculation.

If you'd like to pay your respects to Chief Noah Sealth (Seattle), he's buried in a little cemetery in Suquamish, Washington, across the Puget Sound.

Chief "Seattle," the gentleman who shared his name with Seattle.

I'd become a fan of the Jet City (now Emerald City), partly as a kid watching the old TV show *Here Come the Brides* but mostly because I was a rabid Bruce Lee fan. I knew the martial arts legend had moved to Seattle from Hong Kong as a young man. He attended the University of

★ ★

Washington; opened his first Jeet Kune Do studio in Seattle's Chinatown; met his wife, Linda, at Garfield High School; and was laid to rest beside his son, Brandon, in Lakeview Cemetery, the final resting place of so many of Seattle's historical figures.

When I was asked if I'd like to write this book, it took me about half a nanosecond to decide. Being a history and trivia buff, I've long boasted having a mind that naturally accumulates useless, arcane, but occasionally amusing bits of knowledge. As a Seattle police officer, I've been in a unique position to stumble across some of the most curious people, places, and things this soggy city has produced. I'm about to show you a Seattle you probably don't know—and perhaps never believed existed.

I'm not sure there's a more curious city in America than Seattle. For example, did you know that Seattle was the first American city to win hockey's coveted Stanley Cup? Were you aware that Seattle is home to the only municipally maintained Civil War cemetery in the nation, where more than 200 Union veterans and their wives are buried? And would it surprise you that right across the street, closer than the distance of many of the skirmish lines of Civil War battles, you can find a small burial plot and a memorial to veterans of the Confederate States of America?

This is only a tiny taste of the rich weirdness of this wet, wonderful, and sometimes wacky city called Seattle. Now, come on along—don't forget your bumbershoot—and I'll show you a side of Seattle that'll have people asking why you have that sardonic smirk on your face whenever you drive through the city.

1

North

Areas of a *city can have personalities; I think we can agree on that. However, some areas can be described as having multiple personalities. North Seattle is one of these. As you tour this area you'll find diverse areas, from the Scandinavian-blooded neighborhood of Ballard, which used to be its own city, to the freak show on The AVE (University Way) in the University District, to the place like no other: the legitimate, by city council proclamation Center of the Universe, Fremont (where, curiously, people like to get naked in public—often while riding bikes. Ouch!).*

In the north end you'll find a defunct World War II Navy airbase, one of the finest public universities in the nation, and a commercial fishing fleet that catches 50 percent of all fish caught in the United States, all within mere miles of one another.

Trivia

If you're planning on having a heart attack, Seattle has the reputation as the best U.S. city in which to have one. It's estimated that more than half the adult population of Seattle and King County have had at least some CPR training.

★ ★

The Dawg House
University of Washington

My son Bryan cringes when I have anything good to say about U-Dub. Having attended Washington State University, he's a solid "Coug." However, something he hates even more is when I remind him that when he was a little tyke, whenever he'd see the Huskies on TV, he'd run up and down the front walkway yelling, "Huk-ski games! Huk-ski games!" (Sorry Bry.) And by the time you lay your eyes on these pages, my daughter may be calling herself a Husky—should make holiday dinners lively.

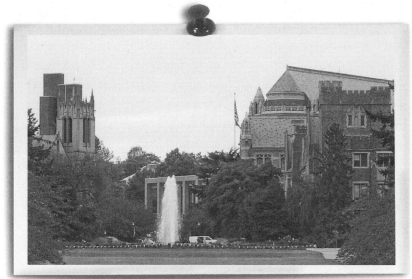

Originally founded in downtown Seattle, today's extraordinary University of Washington campus was a happy by-product of the Alaska-Yukon-Pacific Exposition of 1909.

The University of Washington (UW), founded in 1861, perennially ranks high even when compared with the best private institutions of higher learning across the country and boasts some of the best athletics in the nation. While football, basketball, and baseball may get more attention, there is one sport at UW that deserves a special mention: UW crew.

U-Dub rowers have set a high-water mark for a sport few are aware of. Beginning in 1903 with a win over California, the crew team has gone on to win more than seventy national championships, become the first American sports team to defeat a Soviet team on Soviet Union soil, and won a gold medal at the 1936 Berlin Olympics, defeating Adolph Hitler's German team in epic fashion. In last place at the halfway mark, the UW team rallied in the final 200 meters to win by 8 feet.

The UW campus itself is worth the visit just to stroll around and enjoy its many sights and amenities. The university offers the Burke

The Wave

The Wave is generally accepted to have originated at Husky Stadium on October 31, 1981, during a Washington versus Stanford football game with UW graduate Robb Weller (now of *Entertainment Tonight*) along with UW band director Bill Bissell. Weller's first attempts at The Wave—front row to back row and back row to front row—were flops. With many fans limited to only one hand for balance and the other occupied with a certain hops-and-barley beverage, having to look backward proved hazardous.

Weller was inspired by students' crude attempts in the direction we know today and physically directed the audience to generate a Wave that would flow around the stadium.

Oh, incidentally, the Huskies won that first Wave game, beating Stanford and its quarterback, John Elway, 42–31.

Museum of Natural and Cultural History, contemporary and modern art at the Henry Art Gallery, world-class performances at Meany Hall, the Gallager Law Library, the UW Botanic Gardens for the horticulturally disposed, and, for the ichthyologically inclined, the University of Washington Fish Collection.

The University of Washington is located at 1410 Northeast Campus Parkway. For more information call (206) 543-9198 or visit www .washington.edu.

A Cut Above

Montlake Cut and Bridge

I'd like to tell you that the first thing that comes to mind whenever I drive over the Montlake Bridge is its history, the fact that it's a drawbridge, its beauty, or that logs once traveled through The Cut, which runs beneath it, when it was a mere ditch. I'd like to tell you that, but I can't. Truth be told, there's another, rather morbid memory that pops into my mind.

When I was working as a policeman back in the early 1990s, the department got a call to investigate a person "down" (sick or injured) on the shoreline beneath the Montlake Bridge. Another officer arrived first and found something we hadn't expected: a transient man sitting with his back propped up against a steep bank, his eyes peacefully closed, holding a can of beer—Budweiser, I believe.

Well, it turns out he was about as peaceful as you can get; he was dead. Now that's history you just can't get from a history book.

The Montlake Cut began in 1861 as a log canal that connected Union Bay and Portage Bay. It was basically a ditch dug by Harvey Pike to transport logs to David Denny's Western Lumber Mill. A tram that ran from Lake Washington to Lake Union was used to transport coal from barge to barge.

In 1883 David Denny and Thomas Burke hired Chinese workers to dig a second, larger canal, which was eventually further expanded as a part of the Washington Ship Canal project in 1917.

The first cut isn't always the deepest—it took
three cuts to get to what you see today.

In June 1925 the Montlake Bridge opened to traffic. A bascule-
type drawbridge, this is arguably the most visually pleasing of Seattle's
bridges. It is distinguished by the Gothic styling of its control towers
and light fixtures, arched buttresses, and copper cupolas.

The Montlake Cut and Bridge are located in the 3000 block of
Montlake Boulevard East, immediately south of Husky Stadium on the
southeast portion of the University of Washington campus.

★ ★

Seattle Sun Festival (July 32nd, every year)

Having grown up in New England, I'd never heard of the Seattle Sun Festival. I first learned about this meteorological event when I saw it promoted on a T-shirt: seattle sun festival, july 32nd. An image of a duck wearing sunglasses shared space with the text.

July 32nd is set aside for the arrival, and sadly the immediate departure, of Seattle's summer sun. It doesn't *actually* rain every other day in Seattle—when it's not raining we enjoy a thick, luxurious blanket of clouds.

So now you know Seattle's summer secret: The sun shines only once a year on that special Seattle day, which falls in that mysterious twilight realm after July ends and before August begins. You'll know you've run into a true Seattleite when on that rare day, some tourist in close proximity exclaims, "Look, it's the sun—it's the sun!" and that Seattleite responds, with sympathetic eyes and a cloud-white smile, "Yes, but don't worry, the weatherman says it's gonna rain tomorrow."

Green with Envy
Center for Urban Horticulture

I first learned about this wonderful resource while working in the landscape industry as a foreman for Herron Gardens back in the '80s, before my days on the police force. As the name implies, the center provides classes for professionals and amateurs alike, taught by some of the Northwest's premier master gardeners.

However, the main building, Merrill Hall, stands out for other reasons: It's green. No, not green with envy—it has nothing to envy from buildings built in more traditional fashion. In fact, after seeing this beautiful building, other buildings are more likely to be envious of Merrill Hall.

Founded in 1983, the center suffered a devastating fire in May 2001 that destroyed much of the facility. When rebuilding, designers employed "green" construction technologies. Whether or not you're into that sort of thing, it is a truly fascinating construction method.

Aside from the place being beautiful in appearance, the center utilizes sustainable technologies. For instance, a 2,200-gallon storm-water collection cistern makes the irrigation system more water-efficient, the center is linked to a University of Washington weather station, and builders installed solar panels on the Miller Library roof. The cells provide power sufficient to light the entire main floor.

The Center for Urban Horticulture is located at 3501 Northeast 41st Street. For more information call (206) 543-8616 or visit http://depts .washington.edu/urbhort.

Funny Business
Jet City Improv

If these folks don't qualify as curious, then I'm not sure anyone does. I first discovered the troupe of players several years ago when a good friend of mine, Kyle Kizzier, invited me to a show. Kyle has been a member of the cast for many years—just one of many hats this multi-talented guy wears.

I've always been a fan of improv, but improv is improv, right? You pretty much know what to expect. Wrong! With these guys you never know what to expect. This particular evening of improv had a high-brow twist: It was improvisational Shakespeare.

These versatile folks were hilarious. Breezing through improvisation with a decidedly Shakespearian theme, they kept the packed audience rolling in the aisles.

★ ★

One of the oldest theaters in the city, the Historic University Theater is a fitting home to one of the premier improvisational theater troupes in Seattle: Jet City Improv.

The most recent show I saw was *The Irish Wake*, last St. Patrick's Day. This show had my wife laughing her Irish butt off as she found it reminiscent of her own family.

Created in 1992 by Mike Christensen and Andrew McMasters, the Jet City Improv is now homeported at the Historic University Theater, one of the oldest in the city. They serve beer at the snack bar in the lobby, and there is a bona-fide, honest-to-goodness, no-blarney-here bar right in the theater.

Hey barkeep, pour a wee dram of Jameson's if you don't mind.

The Jet City Improv performs at the Historic University Theater, 5510 University Way NE. For more information call (206) 352-8291 or visit www.jetcityimprov.com.

Bill Nye— More than Just the Science Guy

It seems that "the Science Guy," is a very limited description for Bill Nye, who has accomplished so much more—and then some. Nye's Web site, www. nyelabs.com, is as cool as I'd expected. Even a quick perusal shows that the Science Guy moniker is not sufficient to describe Bill. How about Bill Nye the Professor Guy, or Bill Nye the Inventor Guy, Writer Guy, Comedy Guy, Author Guy, or Engineer Guy; or even Bill Nye the Emmy Award–Winning Guy?

So what am I trying to say about former Boeing engineer, and *Almost Live's* Speed-Walker and a High Fivin' White Guy Bill Nye? That he can't hold a job? Hardly; it's more like he holds so many jobs—at one time. Apparently, Bill is also an avid cyclist. This might explain a personal experience I had back in the mid-1990s with the Bicycle Guy.

I'd just finished sweating my butt up Queen Anne Hill during my Police Mountain Bike training class. We'd stopped for a break at a cafe when we were approached by a *Science Guy* show producer. After obtaining our commander's permission, we officers were filmed in front of our bicycles shouting, "Human Power!" for an episode on human-powered devices. Perhaps you can catch me in a rerun.

Seattle's Favorite Playground
Green Lake

You might be wondering what makes well-known Green Lake a curiosity. Well, first of all, you may not know it as well as you think. But

★ ★

mostly I'm not sure if there's a more popular location in the city for Seattleites of so many varied recreational appetites to gather. Whether you're into a leisurely stroll along one of the lake's two paths, a moderate paddle through the waves, or a vigorous swim, Green Lake Park offers many venues for play. Green Lake also boasts fishing, a kid's playground, soccer and softball fields, basketball and tennis courts, canoe and pedal boat rentals, fishing piers, an indoor swimming pool, and even a chip-and-putt golf course for those wannabe Freddie Couples.

Whenever I think of going to Green Lake on a weekend or on one of our rare sunny days, the wit of Yogi Berra comes to mind. To paraphrase: "No one ever goes to Green Lake; it's always too crowded." This lake has been "green" since it was first surveyed in 1855 by David Phillips, who named it Lake Green. The lake got its name from its proliferation of algae blooms—a condition that causes the infamous Green Lake itch.

Green Lake is unique in that it has no surface water inlets or outlets. Revenna Creek once flowed from Green Lake to Lake Washington, but in order to create more park space, in 1911 the water level was lowered by about 7 feet, causing the creek to dry up. Today the lake is fed exclusively by rain, runoff, and the city water supply.

The east side of the lake was at one time home to a sawmill and a trolley line connecting the lake area with downtown Seattle. Trolleys once completely circumnavigated the lake.

These are just a few interesting facets of this historical area, which still serves as one of the strongest magnets for fun to be found in the city. So grab your picnic basket, in-line skates, bike, running shoes, canoe—oh, and a friend or two—and head on down to Seattle's Green Lake the next time you're feeling a need to sweat. You can sweat simply lying in the sun on Green Lake's sandy beach, too!

The intersection of East Green Lake Way North and North 65th Street is a good place to reach the lake. From there you can go north or south around the lake.

★ ★

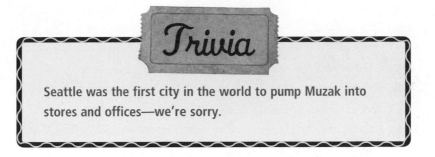

Trivia

Seattle was the first city in the world to pump Muzak into stores and offices—we're sorry.

The Wettest Show on Earth

Aqua Theater

This one will be especially interesting to anyone who has ever walked, run, or rolled past the big, ugly concrete thing (no, not the Kingdome; that's gone) that's been hunkering at the south end of Green Lake for decades. The cement-gray skeleton is what remains of grandstands that once provided seats for more than 5,500 fans to watch spectacular performances on the lake.

The Aqua Follies inaugurated the Aqua Theater with a show during the first Sea Fair event, on August 11, 1950. In a city known for water in every direction you turn your head, the Aqua Follies were nationally famous, locally popular, and a perfect fit for Seattle. The theater also attracted other national acts, from Bob Hope to the Grateful Dead, who in 1969 performed one of the last shows held at the Aqua Theater before it closed.

The Aqua Follies performers were a group of women on water skis, like you've seen in those film clips from the '50s and '60s, climbing on top of one another and performing various formations and tricks most of us couldn't do in our dreams.

The 1962 World's Fair saw the Aqua Theater rise to the height of its popularity. With so many visitors from around the nation in Seattle for the fair, the theater attracted a plethora of national performers and productions to the watery venue. One unique attraction of the venue was its floating orchestra pit.

★ ★

The Aqua Theater is perfectly named—I mean, what other kind of theater belongs in Seattle?

Sadly, water coming from the sky, which is fundamental to Seattle's personality, especially for outsiders, doomed the Aqua Theater. Even in late summer, Seattle rain can be unpredictable, and attendees tired of canceled shows and huddling under umbrellas during rain showers. The Aqua Follies ended in 1964, and the city eventually closed the facility.

Rooster Tails to Crow About

Thunderboats

The Chevrolet (or various incarnations over the years) Cup at the Seafair Hydroplane Races, held on Lake Washington in Seattle every summer, is as well-known as the races are well attended. However, although hydroplane racing in the Emerald City goes back at least half a century, the venue wasn't always as roomy as it is now.

Well before Lake Washington became the Thunderboat capital it has come to be, its much smaller but similarly popular cousin to the west, Green Lake, was the place for Seattle hydroplane racing. In fact, in 1975 Green Lake actually hosted a world hydroplane racing championship. The modest-size lake hosted the prestigious Heidleberg Inboard World Championships, considered the premier limited inboard event on Earth.

More than one hundred boats from all over America ripped up the 1⅔-mile oval course in excess of 100 miles per hour. This fan-friendly free event attracted more than 100,000 people over the course of the three-day competition.

Races involving other classes of boats were also held, with winners receiving trophies or other prizes. The Green Lake course was considered the fastest boat-racing course of its kind. Evidence of this claim is the fact that Green Lake boasted more speed records than any other racecourse in the world.

Think about this next time you walk, run, or bike around the Green Lake path, staring at the little ol' lake: In one exhibition race, boats blasted across the lake in a quarter-mile sprint at nearly 200 miles per hour. The Seafair hydros remained at Green Lake through the 1976 racing season.

For more information on the races and other Seafair Festival activities, visit www.seafair.com.

★ ★

The Great Seattle Slug

Believe it or not, some folks don't like these yucky little critters, which are basically shell-less snails. Many gardeners use slug bait to kill them, but slug bait is also poisonous to pets, fish, and humans. So here's a unique solution—although for some of you this process will represent a sacrifice, or even sacrilege, as a beer offering is involved.

In the evening, place a bowl of beer out where your herd of slugs grazes. In the morning you're likely to find several slugs suffering the ramifications of their final binge. By the way, the darker the beer the better.

Getting back to the slime factor for a moment, every Seattleite has seen many a slime trail—a slug's version of dropping breadcrumbs to find one's way back. Slugs return along their slime trails to relocate good hunting/feeding locations.

One fact sheet on slugs states that wet conditions are ideal for slug development. Translation: Seattle is ideal for slug development. As for that development, slugs grow to amazing proportions, up to 7 inches long, and it feels like you're stepping on an overripe banana when you squish one between your bare toes.

Lions and Tigers and Deer—Oh, My!
Woodland Park Zoo

When we first moved to Seattle, we had no family to visit on holidays such as Thanksgiving and Christmas. Now, with three children, the five of us made a half-decent-size family in our own right; but what we needed for after the kids had opened their presents from Santa was a good old-fashioned family tradition. When we learned that the Woodland Park Zoo offered half-price admission on Christmas Day, we had found our new Christmas tradition.

We found even more surprises at the zoo on Christmas with complimentary hot chocolate, hot apple cider, and cookies. What a deal! Despite the drizzle, we had a spectacular time. The zoo is a treat without these extra amenities; with them, it made our first Christmas away from New England something special. Sadly, the zoo eventually discontinued the half-price admission and free goodies on Christmas Day, and thus ended our family's new tradition. We still love the zoo, though. Each of us visits at least once a year, separately or together, although not always on Christmas Day.

The zoo, part of Woodland Park, unofficially began with a few deer on the shores of Green Lake in the late nineteenth century. Anglo-American Guy Phinney, adhering to his aristocratic English traditions, established a deer park on his estate on the eastern slope of what today is known as Phinney Ridge. By the time Phinney died in 1893, a small herd of deer roamed the area.

Seattle's first zoo was actually a small collection of animals residing at Leschi Park. These animals were donated to Seattle after the city purchased Phinney's Woodland Park estate. When the Olmstead Brothers of Boston, creators of New York's Central Park, designed an integrated park system throughout Seattle, they included converting Phinney's estate into a park.

After many years of often bland, diorama-style exhibits, the 1980s saw a dramatic leap toward a more natural environment for the animals. Today's exhibits include an Asian elephant habitat, a tropical rain forest, the Northern Trail, the African Savannah, African Wild Dog, Jaguar Cove, and way too much more to name them all. The complex also contains an education center, a zoo store, and an animal health complex.

Nearby Carkeek Park's original use was as a vegetable garden to grow food for the zoo animals.

Woodland Park Zoo is located at 5500 Phinney Avenue North. For more information phone (206) 684-4800 or visit www.zoo.org.

He Brought the Brides

Nothing about Seattle history would be considered complete without a mention of Asa Mercer, one of the three Mercer brothers who helped settle Seattle. Although his surname brings to mind an island-city near Seattle as well as a major Seattle street (aka, at rush hour, the Mercer Mess), those things were actually named for his brother, Thomas.

Asa Mercer did accomplish a lot, however. He was the University of Washington's first president, as well as its first professor, and was later elected to the Washington Territory Senate. However, it was something else that brought him a singular fame: Asa Mercer brought women to Seattle. Woo-hoo!

At the time, Seattle had one potential wife for every nine prospective husbands. A crafty opportunist, Asa observed that New England had a surplus of promising brides, as hubby prospects were away fighting the Civil War.

On May 16, 1864, Asa returned to Seattle with the first eleven potential brides. The loggers were understandably thrilled. I imagine the women's sentiments were something else entirely.

The Scandinavian Riviera
Ballard

Located in northwest Seattle, Ballard has one of the most distinctive personalities of any neighborhood in Seattle. How can it not, considering that in 1887 Capt. William Rankin Ballard reportedly acquired the 160 acres of land that became Ballard when he lost a coin toss for the "undesirable" parcel?

The city of Ballard's early rise and fall can be summed up by fire and water. After the Great Seattle Fire of 1889, two newly built mills in Ballard, one for lumber and the other producing shingles, created products necessary for rebuilding Seattle. Ballard's busy mills were attracting so many residents that it incorporated as a city in 1890.

It's hard to imagine that too little water would ever be a problem anywhere in the Seattle area, but that was the precise problem Ballard faced in the early 1900s. Ballard couldn't provide sufficient drinking water to its citizens, forcing a vote on annexation by Seattle. The vote failed, and Ballard continued to obtain its water through a tense water-sharing agreement with Seattle. However, in 1906 the Washington State Supreme Court ruled that Seattle was not obligated to share its water resources with neighboring cities. Water restrictions forced a subsequent vote, and in 1907 Ballard became Seattle's newest neighborhood.

Ballard is best known for its Scandinavian heritage. You can't go 2 blocks without seeing a Nordic name: Viking Tavern, Swedish Club, Sons of Norway, Danish flags, Viking Sport Seattle Cycling Team, etc. The community also celebrates Norwegian Constitution Day, and the slogan of the 2007 Ballard Seafood Fest was "Feed Your Inner Viking."

King Olav's Piece of Ballard
Bergen Place Park

Bergen Place Park honors the 1967 sister-city relationship between the people of Seattle and the people of Bergen, Norway. In 1975 the park was dedicated to King Olav of Norway.

★ ★

I Told My Legs to Stop, but . . .

The Goodwill Games came to Seattle in summer 1990. It's obvious to compare these games with the Olympics, but one thing that separated the two was the former's broader scope. Arts and cultural exhibitions were included, making the Goodwill Games more of a festival than exclusively a sporting event.

The Seattle games were special for many other reasons as well, but they were especially poignant for me. Why? It could have been because several world records were broken during the event, but it wasn't. It could have been because Kristi Yamaguchi won a figure skating gold medal, defeating the reigning world champion, but it wasn't. It could even have been because the games witnessed an amazing race between American teammates Carl Lewis and Leroy Burrell, which Burrell won, but it wasn't that, either.

Nope, it was poignant for me because the Goodwill Games Marathon offered a citizens category in which I competed (I use that term very loosely). About three and a half hours after the starting gun, which I

The city of Bergen was founded slightly earlier than its American sister—like 800 years earlier, in 1070. Bergen is described as having "a temperate climate with frequent rain." (Remind you of anyplace?) Also, similar to the seven hills Seattle is built on, Bergen is built on seven "mountains"; and while Seattle is known as the gateway to Alaska and Asia, Bergen is known as a gateway to the fjords and Europe.

The tree- and bench-lined park is located in a triangle of land in the

was too far back in the throng to hear, I proudly—perhaps mirac-
ulously—completed the course. Including a "citizens" category
allowing the average person to compete in the marathon was
another thing that set the Goodwill Games apart from the Olympics
and is something I will never forget.

Certain things cling to my memory about that day, aside from eventually losing two toenails and crashing to sleep on my couch until
the next morning: One was the heat; runners baked in temperatures
that hovered in the low to mid-90s that day. Another thing was the
debate raging between my legs and my mind as we passed mile 17
or so, crossing the Ballard Bridge—each begging the other to quit,
each ignoring the other.

I also need to comment on the description of the marathon winners as elite endurance athletes. Winner Dave Mora of the United
States finished at 2:14:49:27. I, on the other hand, was still out on
the course in oppressive heat an hour and a half later, while Dave
and his elite buddies were probably drinking beer and eating pizza.
Now let me ask you, who is really the endurance athlete?

heart of Ballard, Seattle's Scandinavian enclave, between Leary Avenue
NW and Northwest Market Street on 22nd Avenue NW. The trees,
however, aren't your common variety. Called *The Witness Trees,* they
are the work of artist Jenn Lee Dixon.

Bergen Place Park is located at 5420 22nd Avenue NW. For more
information call (206) 684-4075 or visit http://seattle.gov/parks/
parkdetail.asp?ID=253.

★ ★

Jerry Garcia Slept Here
Golden Gardens Park

Okay, well maybe he didn't sleep here—perhaps a catnap between sets—but he did play his music here. I'm betting you didn't know that about Ballard's eighty-eight-acre Golden Gardens Park. Even if you did, you probably wouldn't have been aware of this little tidbit: The Grateful Dead actually played Golden Gardens in July 1967—powered by generator—from the back of a flatbed truck at a San Francisco–styled "hippie" event called the "Be-In."

Now that we've got perhaps the oddest—albeit, coolest—fact about the park out of the way, let me tell you a bit about one of Seattle's city park gems. Located on the shores of Puget Sound, the park offers incredible Olympic Mountain views. The park also offers hiking trails through dense forest and along primitive shoreline, a fishing pier, and boat rentals. You can also rent the 1930s-era bathhouse for your special event. Don't forget Fido or Spot—the park features one of the city's off-leash dog areas.

While it's best to avoid most city parks by night, Golden Gardens is different. It offers five open-fire pits on the beach, which are allotted on a first-come, first-served basis. On a related but more humorous note: The current mayor of Seattle, a self-styled "green" warrior, attempted to outlaw these beach fire pits, but cooler heads prevailed. As of this writing at least, fire pit fires are still permitted. But be sure to bring your own firewood—burning driftwood found on the beach is a no-no.

Golden Gardens Park is located at 8498 Seaview Place NW. For more information call (206) 684-4075 or visit www.seattle.gov/parks/parkdetail.asp?ID=243.

From Rail to Trail
Burke-Gilman Trail

Jody and I know the Burke-Gilman Trail very well, and I suppose our children wish they didn't. In fact, we think they've been conspiring to see if any charges could still be brought against us for what they term "child abuse" for the number of times we took them for long walks or bike rides.

We used the trail for casual walking and cycling excursions as well as to train for the Goodwill Games marathon and the Seattle half marathons. We still use the path regularly, but today it's more for the casual walk or ride than the hair-on-fire, screaming-for-the-pain-to-stop training we used to do. I doubt our children will ever bring their own kids anywhere near the place.

The Burke-Gilman Trail begins in Seattle's Ballard neighborhood and follows the old Lake Shore & Eastern Railroad tracks along the Ship Canal, Lake Union, and then north along Lake Washington's western shores. The Burke-Gilman portion of the trail ends at Blyth Park in Bothell, but the trail itself continues east to Marymoor Park in Redmond as the Sammamish River Trail.

Keep in mind that this trail is shared by cyclists as well as foot traffic. Most cyclists are considerate, but be on the lookout for those who aren't.

The Burke-Gilman/Sammamish River Trail is accessible at several points along nearly its entire length, which is 27 miles combined. There are several points along the path for your food and beverage needs. Bike shops are located conveniently near the trail in the University District, Bothell, and Redmond.

For more information on the Burke-Gilman Trail, visit www .cityofseattle.net/parks/BurkeGilman/bgtrail.htm.

Hello Ocean, Meet the Lakes
Ballard Locks

No, the Hiram M. Chittenden Locks, known to Seattleites as the Ballard Locks, are not the kind eaten for breakfast with bagels and cream cheese. This despite the fact that the Ballard Locks are home to a fish ladder that allows salmon to migrate into Lake Washington.

The U.S. Army Corps of Engineers built these non-edible locks and dedicated the facility on July 4, 1917. (It seems Seattle had a thing for Independence Day dedications; the Smith Tower was dedicated on this holiday a few years earlier.) The locks are composed of two holding pens: one small, 30 by 150 feet, for smaller boats and use in summer when marine traffic is low to conserve fresh water in Lake Union; the other, 80 by 825 feet, for large vessels.

The locks were built to move boats from the water level of Puget Sound to the water level of Lakes Union and Washington and back again. The facility maintains a lake water level at 20.6 feet above the sound's mean low tide and prevents saltwater intrusion into the freshwater lakes. Not sure why they didn't use the sound's pleasant low tide, but I'm no scientist.

The dedication ceremony's flagship, the S.S. *Roosevelt,* the ship that carried Admiral Peary on his North Pole expedition, led a 300-craft flotilla through the locks and remainder of the Lake Washington Ship Canal. By the time of this dedication, the locks had been in operation since February 5, 1916, with 17,000 vessels having floated through it to Lake Washington.

If you spend some time at this facility, you won't be disappointed. From the nearby Carl S. English Jr. Botanical Garden to Seattle's fishing fleet moored in the background, you won't find a more picturesque place in the city.

The Hiram M. Chittenden (Ballard) Locks are located at 3015 Northwest 54th Street. For more information call (206) 783-7059 or visit www.nws.usace.army.mil/PublicMenu/Menu.cfm?sitename=lwsc&page name=mainpage.

The Ballard Locks allow both fish and fishermen through. I think I know who got the better deal here.

The Case of the Purloining Pinnipeds

Back in the 1980s, seagoing squatters in search of a seafood buffet found one at the Ballard Locks. Herschel, the lovable to some and detestable to others California sea lion, apparently preferred Washington. Herschel and company caused the salmon run to decline to as few as seventy fish.

Elusive and cunning, the critter confounded those tasked with his eviction; seems Herschel wasn't about to come home to find his furniture set out on the dock. The supercilious sea lion scoffed at various noise-makers, and state wildlife staff didn't fool him when they introduced a plastic killer whale.

Herschel had fans in Seattle, but the salmon were not among them. Herschel and his buddies—Hondo, Bob, and Big Frank—had an insatiable taste for sushi. Fish and game professionals finally extradited the Herschel clan to California. Seattle's schoolchildren may have been disappointed, but the salmon were relieved.

No one knows what became of Herschel after his move to sunny California. He has probably linked up with another group of flipper-flappin' ne'er-do-wells and continues his fish-chompin' ways today.

Deadliest Catch's Homeport
Fisherman's Terminal

For almost a century, Seattle's Fisherman's Terminal, which is operated by the Port of Seattle, has been home to the North Pacific's commercial

Seattle's Fisherman's Terminal is where many of the rugged men and women who fish the North Pacific moor their boats, including those seen on the Discovery Channel's *Deadliest Catch*.

fishing fleet. Located just east of the Ballard Locks and west of the Ballard Bridge, the terminal provides freshwater mooring for fishing vessels and pleasure craft, with preference given to working boats.

The terminal has more than 225,000 square feet of retail, light industrial, warehouse, and office space. The facility serves over 600 vessels up to 250 feet long. There is also short-term public mooring for up to four hours.

If you've ever watched the Discovery Channel's popular series *Deadliest Catch,* you've no doubt seen some of the many fishing boats that call Fisherman's Terminal home. The show captures the adventures of commercial fishing vessels and their crews as they brave the most dangerous working conditions on Earth just to put seafood on your table.

The terminal is also one of the most picturesque locations in Seattle. That's saying a lot for a city known for its picturesque-ness. You can easily spend hours here just staring at the myriad fishing boats and pleasure craft, some beautiful, others merely functional.

The danger of the job hits you when you stop to reflect at the Fisherman's Memorial—a stone and bronze monument emblazoned with plaques dedicated to the more than 500 men and women lost to the sea over the past one hundred years.

Fisherman's Terminal is located at 3919 18th Avenue West. For more information call (206) 728-3395 or visit www.portseattle.org/seaport/marinas/fishermensterminal.

"De Libertas Quirkas"
Fremont

Whenever I mention the Fremont neighborhood to non-Fremonter Seattleites, I'm as likely to get a smile and a pleasant "mmmm" as I am to get an eye roll and a "hrumphh." It's easy to say each neighborhood of this city is unique, because Seattle is unique. However, Fremont stands alone in its uniqueness. In fact, this artsy—without the fartsy—semi-hippie haven, semi-entrepreneurial enclave is downright quirky and peculiar.

Well, considering that Fremont's motto is "De Libertas Quirkas," which means "Free to Be Peculiar," I'd say my description fits to a T—a tie-dyed T that is. For such a small neighborhood, Fremont has a great deal to offer. In fact, you'll find several separate entries on Fremont's fascinating stuff.

You can visit the *Fremont Troll,* a statue of Lenin (not John, Vlad), the *Fremont Rocket,* and the *Waiting for the Interurban* sculpture, which, despite Fremonters' naked proclivities, they're constantly dressing up in all manner of clothing.

If you come at the right time of year, take in the Solstice Parade. Since many participants, remaining consistent with a theme, prefer to ride their bikes in the buff, I'll let you guess which solstice—summer or winter—warrants the celebration.

Perhaps the first thing you need to know about Fremont is that it is the certified Center of the Universe. Stop laughing; it's true! An official decree of the Seattle City Council proclaimed Fremont the Center of the Universe, a mystical notion originally passed down by local Indians.

Fremont is located in northwest Seattle. For more information on the neighborhood, visit www.fremontseattle.com.

The Happy Little Bridge

Fremont Bridge

You know how it is. You zip past or over a structure so often as a part of your daily commute that you may never know you're passing over history. This is the case with the landmark Fremont Bridge. I'm not sure what it is. Seattle has many drawbridges, but for some reason I've always thought Fremont's was the quaintest. Perhaps it's the color. It was originally painted bright orange, distinguishing it from other drawbridges in the city. Unfortunately the orange faded too quickly, so today the bridge is painted blue—still different from the other city bridges, which are bridge-green—with orange accents as a nod to its past hue.

This bridge may be little, straddling the Lake Washington Ship Canal since 1917, but over the years it's been the busiest drawbridge in Seattle and one of the busiest bascule drawbridges in the world. (In case you're wondering, a bascule bridge has a bridge surface, or "leaf," that's raised and lowered by counterweight balancing housed in concrete piers topped with towers.) The bridge opens (and closes) approximately thirty-five times daily, and as of September 20, 1991, the bridge had opened half a million times.

★ ★

This quaint bridge leads to Fremont—the city-proclaimed Center of the Universe.

I think what I like most about this drawbridge is the way it spills traffic and pedestrians right into the heart of Fremont's primary business district. So when headed into or out of Fremont, a place where there is so much else to see, don't neglect the little drawbridge that carries you over the canal.

The Fremont Bridge is located between Westlake and Nickerson Avenues North at Fourth Avenue North on Queen Anne Hill and North 34th Street at Fremont Avenue North in Fremont.

Betcha' Didn't Know

Aurora Bridge

Okay, how many of you know the Aurora Bridge's true name? Tourists and newcomers to Seattle may be excused, but most Seattleites I

★ ★

spoke to, as well as yours truly, had no clue that its actual name is the George Washington Memorial Bridge.

The Aurora Bridge got its common name because it carries Aurora Avenue (Highway 99) across the ship canal from Queen Anne Hill to Fremont. The state officially dedicated the bridge on February 22, 1932—George Washington's 200th birthday—and the bridge was listed on the National Register of Historic Places in 1982.

The Aurora Bridge has a dubious distinction: Seattle is nationally famous for its high per capita suicide rate, and the bridge is locally famous as the place where many of the suicidal choose to make a final 167-foot leap as they bid adieu to this cruel world. In fact, the first person to dive to his death didn't bother to wait for construction to be finished. He jumped off the incomplete structure in January 1932. Due to this bridge having become a destination of the depressed, the State of Washington, which owns the bridge, has installed several phones and even more signs urging those contemplating a jump to reconsider and instead call for help.

Seattleites can't talk about the bridge without mentioning its most tragic incident. Back in November 1998, Silas Cool shot Metro Transit bus driver Mark McLaughlin as he drove southbound on the Aurora Bridge. As a result, the coach veered across the bridge and plunged over the side onto the roof of an apartment building. Amazingly, only three deaths resulted: the driver, one passenger, and Cool, who shot himself. Metro Transit has since retired Route 359.

The Aurora Bridge is located roughly at Aurora Avenue North from Halladay Street (Queen Anne Hill) to North 38th Street (Fremont).

Madame Mayor—In 1926?

Seattle has several firsts in America, which is amazing considering its relative youth. One auspicious honor: In 1926 Seattle elected the first female mayor of a major city in the United States' history.

Bertha Knight Landes, daughter of a Union Civil War veteran, was born in Ware, Massachusetts, in 1868; received a degree from Indiana University in 1891; and moved to Seattle with her husband in 1895.

Mayor Landes's mission was to clean up government. Although successful, that success seemed irrelevant at reelection. The prevailing sentiment at the time benefited her well-funded opponent, a political unknown named Frank Edwards.

Seems folks preferred a man to run a large, growing city such as Seattle. However, they may have been better off with a less misogynistic point of view. Edwards was recalled by voters amid cries of corruption, having miffed voters by apparently favoring certain private-interest groups.

After leaving city politics, Landes remained involved in many organizations, often serving in a leadership capacity. Prior to becoming mayor, she was the only woman appointed by the mayor to a five-member commission to study joblessness. She later became a charter member of Seattle Soroptimists, a professional women's group, and later was elected its president.

Bertha Landes died in 1943.

* *

Clothes? Bah! Who Needs Clothes?

Solstice Parade

Mention the Solstice Parade to anyone who's been in Seattle for any length of time and you'll likely hear one response: naked cyclists.

The Summer Solstice Parade and Pageant has earned its place as unique among the unique. One thing that sets it apart, aside from some parade participants' proclivity for pedaling in the buff, is an eccentric set of rules established for the parade. According to the Fremont Arts Council:

- No printed words or logos
- No live animals (Guide animals are exempted.)
- No motorized vehicles
- No real weapons
- No advertisements during the parade

I have to give parade organizers credit, though; even they describe the parade as "weird." As with so many other things in Seattle, the focus is on "hands-on" participation. Anyone and everyone willing to adhere to the rules above are invited to participate in the parade.

Following the parade, organizers invite folks to walk or ride (often still naked, so be advised if you're bringing the kiddies) to Gas Works Park to listen to music until sundown, which at summer solstice can be quite late indeed.

Ready, Aim . . . Fire!

The Fremont Rocket

Just when you thought you'd seen it all in Fremont, there's more. But really, can you have too much of anything in the bona-fide Center of the Universe? It seems appropriate that the universal nexus should pay homage to space travel. That's right; at 617 North 35th Street you'll find a former Cold War–era missile, and current sculpture, *The Fremont Rocket*.

★ ★

During a tiff with city leaders, Fremonters actually aimed their rocket at City Hall, threatening Fremont's reputation as a peaceful hippy-haven. Heather Pomper

The 53-foot rocket, a remnant of the Cold War, is a refugee from a surplus store in Belltown. When members of the Fremont Business Association, who'd been busting their brains for something unique to stamp Fremont even more indelibly on the map, heard that a surplus missile had become available, they acted immediately. No scrapyard for this prodigious projectile—no sir, this was just weird enough to do the trick. In 1993 a team headed by rocket scientist Warner Von Hoge completely rebuilt the rocket and erected it just in time for the 1994 Solstice Parade.

Fremont's motto, "De Libertas Quirkas"—"Freedom to Be Peculiar"—is emblazoned on the fuselage. The rocket's nose and fins bear neon lasers, and when in "launch mode," the rocket's base emits steam vapors.

It's also proved quite practical at times. In fact, as reported in the *Seattle Times,* while embroiled in a neighborhood boundary issue some years back, residents of Fremont, alternately known as Fremonsters, actually aimed the rocket at City Hall. Fortunately the city backed down and a Bay of Ducks crisis was averted.

The Fremont Rocket is located at Evanston Avenue North and North 36th Street in Fremont.

No Flatulence Here
Gas Works Park

This nineteen-acre-plus-a-big-lawn-size park may be the strangest public park in Seattle. It's not just that an old gasworks plant is an unlikely place to build a park and playground. Retaining the massive, rusted and cracking towers (large cylinders where chemical reactions take place) instead of razing them also pushes the design envelope.

Opened in 1906, the Seattle Gas Light Company provided much-needed energy to Seattleites. The plant puffed smoke into the skies over Lake Union until 1956, when the ability to import natural gas made the plant obsolete and ended an era.

In 1962 the City of Seattle purchased the property, but it wasn't until 1975 that Gas Works Park opened to the public. The park was designed by Richard Hagg, a University of Washington architecture and planning professor, who developed a personal attachment to the

★ ★

Go fly a kite! No, really! Gas Works Park is one of the best places in Seattle to fly a kite.

original rust-coated towers and the surrounding apparatus that dominate the park. Today the cracking towers and other original structures give the park its distinctive character. Hagg was so successful in integrating the old, original structures with the new that he was awarded the American Society of Landscape Architects President's Award of Design Excellence.

From the shores of Lake Union, a large grassy expanse rises toward a man-made knoll called Kite Hill, upon which a path wends its way to a magnificent sundial embedded at the summit. The park serves as an inviting picnic stop on the way to Ballard or to Log Boom Park in Kenmore to the northeast.

Anyone Got the Time?

When you're finished taking in the beautiful views of Lake Union and its marinas, the Seattle skyline, and the old rusty gasworks structures, turn your eyes toward the park's high point, called Kite Hill.

What you're looking for is an intricate and artful sundial embedded into the crown of the man-made emerald-green knoll. In 1978 Charles Greening, assisted by Kim Lazare, created the multimedia sundial out of concrete, brass, shells, and glass. You can tread up the grassy slope, but if it's wet you might want to stay on the paved goat trail. Otherwise you may find yourself back at the base of the hill on your butt.

Your first thought may be, *How the heck does this thing work?* There's no protrusion to cast a shadow in order to tell time—well, until you arrive. The most unique thing about this sundial is that it won't work without you. Talk about interactive; near the sundial you'll find a plaque with instructions for completing the mechanism, with *you* being the only moving part. One o'clock—nice work!

The sundial is located atop Kite Hill in Gas Works Park, 2101 North Northlake Way. For more information call (206) 684-4075 or visit www.seattle.gov/parks/park_detail .asp?id=293.

Got the time? Climbing the hill to get it will be well worth the hike.

Along with a spectacular Fourth of July fireworks display, the park is also the destination of the often-naked solstice cyclists following the Fremont Solstice Parade. And appropriately, it's the Seattle venue for folks who make no pretensions about riding in the buff: the World Naked Bike Ride, another clothes-free cycling event in the Emerald City.

Gas Works Park is located at 2101 North Northlake Way in Fremont. For more information call (206) 684-4075 or visit www.seattle.gov/parks/park_detail.asp?id=293.

You Can Dress 'Em Up, but...
Waiting for the Interurban

In 1979 artist Richard Beyer created a sculpture that would, from that day forward, allow others to express their own creative notions. Due to its location and accessibility on a traffic island at the busy intersection of North 34th Street and Fremont Avenue North, just north of the Fremont Bridge, *Waiting for the Interurban* is Fremont's most popular attraction and one of the most popular in the city.

Beyer created the cast-aluminum sculpture of five people and one dog (with a human face) standing beneath a transit shelter waiting, well, waiting for the Interurban—which, by the way, isn't comin'. The Interurban was an early-twentieth-century rail line that connected Seattle to its various neighborhoods and to neighboring cities.

This sculpture allows folks to express their creativity by dressing up the remarkably imperturbable rail passengers. Over the years folks have dressed the statue in almost every manner imaginable. I trust you'll come up with something unique.

There is actually an official protocol regulating statue adornment or bedecking them with the proper accoutrement. In fact there are five. I'm going to paraphrase for space considerations, but these are gleaned from www.FremontSeattle.com:

1. Be polite.

These patient potential passengers have been waiting for years for a train that ran its last run long ago. You can dress them up, but don't try to take them out; they weigh a ton.

2. First come, first decorate. (If current decorations appear fresh, leave them.)
3. No advertising.
4. Return to take down decorations.
5. Be polite.

If you aren't satisfied to bask in your own private artistic glory, go ahead and photograph your masterpiece and send it to the History House, 790 North 34th Street, Seattle, WA 98103.

Good Luck!

Waiting for the Interurban is located at North 34th Street and Fremont Avenue North in Fremont.

Trolling Fremont
The Fremont Troll

During our first admiration-fest of Fremont's most enigmatic resident—well, inanimate resident anyway—my wife asked me, "Why would they put it here?" pointing to the space where the sculpture had been wedged. I said, "Where else would a troll reside other than under a bridge?"

The Fremont Troll is Seattle's favorite under-bridge-residing, VW-huggin' denizen. Jason Woering

Remember the Norwegian folktale "Three Billy Goats Gruff"? Since trollologists teach us that trolls don't tolerate sunshine very well, what better place than Seattle to lurk?

The mixed-media giant appears to be clawing its way out of the earth into its niche beneath the Aurora Bridge on the north side of North 36th Street at Troll Avenue North. The most intriguing aspect of the sculpture is what the troll has clutched in its left hand: an actual VW Beetle. Incidentally, the doomed bug originally had a California license plate.

After winning a competition held by the Fremont Arts Council, local artists Steve Badanes, Will Martin, Donna Walter, and Ross Whitehead spent seven weeks sculpting the two-ton megalith out of reinforced ferroconcrete. With interactivity in mind, they encourage folks to clamber, skitter, and otherwise scramble over and about the Fremont Troll.

The troll's copyright is commercially protected, so do some research before pasting its handsome mug on your latest snake oil, widget, or better mousetrap. Entrepreneurs don't despair: *The Fremont Troll* does appear on some commercial products—among them, Troll Porter, offered by Hale's Ales, a Fremont microbrewery.

The Fremont Troll dwells under the Aurora Bridge at North 36th Street and Troll Avenue North.

I Don't Know Either, but There It Is

Statue of Lenin

This bronze remnant of the Soviet era evokes strong responses from some who view it, especially those who had escaped the brutal communist regime. Others, those without the personal history connection, may consider its purely artistic elements, which are impressive indeed.

The Soviets commissioned Emil Venkov to create the 16-foot statue of Vladimir Lenin. In 1988, after ten years' work, the statue was erected in Poprad, Slovakia. Summarily toppled when the Soviet Union collapsed, the work was left to wallow in the mud.

Lewis Carpenter, an American from the Seattle area who was teaching in Poprad at the time, recognized the historical value of the massive bronze statue or, failing that, its huge value as seven tons of scrap metal. He mortgaged his house and purchased ol' Vlad for $41,000

★ ★

**Why Lenin? Don't ask. Just look around for a while—
this is Fremont after all.** Heather Pomper

and shipped the piece to Seattle. Actually it went first to nearby
Issaquah, where he kept the metal dictator in his yard—talk about a
lawn jockey on steroids!

Sadly Carpenter was killed in a car wreck only days after returning to Seattle, and his estate has owned the statue ever since. Vlad's
been on display at various locations but now stands in Fremont at the
intersection of Evanston Avenue North, North 36th Street, and Fremont
Place in front of a Taco Del Mar restaurant.

Over the years the statue has suffered such indignities as being
decorated with lights at Christmas, made to impersonate John Lennon,
dressed in drag during Gay Pride Week, painted as a clown, and having any number of signs hung from him proclaiming everything under
the sun.

Many folks believe this is the only statue of Lenin that displays him
as a violent revolutionary rather than an intellectual and philosopher.
Perhaps this was something Emil Venkov snuck by the Soviet propa-
gandists who thought the statue portrayed Vlad as a warrior, when
the intent was to show him as the tyrant history has shown him to
be—who knows.

Organic, Free Trade, and Danged Delicious

Theo's Chocolate Factory

Visiting some of these Seattle curiosities has been a real treat. With
Theo's Chocolate Factory, I mean "treat" in a deliciously literal way.

When Jody and I arrived at Theo's Chocolate Factory, located in
the former Redhook Brewery building in Fremont, we were met by
the delightful Debra Music, VP of sales and marketing. I explained to
Deb that I'd be writing tidbits about cool Seattle stuff that would whet
folks' appetite to visit or learn more.

I told Deb that I could simply write, "They have chocolate!" and my
job would be done. Deb agreed but added, "We have free chocolate!"
Boy is that true—and how. We weren't with Deb for more than three
seconds before she offered us heavenly samples, which are distributed
liberally to guests during daily tours.

The folks at Theo's have a passion not only for producing deli-
cious gourmet chocolate but also for doing it in what they regard as a

★ ★

Aside from being yummy, Theo's chocolates are organic and a product of fair-trade deals with farm co-ops.

socially and environmentally conscientious manner. Theo's is committed to purchasing cacao beans from farmers who participate in fair-trade agreements as members of democratic farm cooperatives that engage in sustainable farming techniques. Fair-trade agreements are designed to promote worker welfare, minimize environmental harm, and assist producers in increasing their profits, thereby raising the standards of living for all involved.

Like so many entrepreneurs, founder Joe Whinney took a risk on a belief in a business venture, even moving from Boston to Seattle. And like some of those risk takers, he forged into a business where none had gone before, becoming the first person in the United States to import organic cacao beans.

Deb mentioned that the importing didn't go unnoticed. Being the first of its kind, authorities flagged the container for scrutiny until they determined it wasn't holding an illicit drug but rather the quite licit, although equally addictive, precursor to chocolate.

Stop by sometime; you won't believe the amazing selection of chocolate you'll find available for purchase. If you would like to find out more about this unique enterprise, give them a call to be included on an informative tour. Believe me, they'd love to tell you more about what they do.

Theo's Chocolate Factory is located at 3400 Phinney Avenue North, Fremont. For more information or to schedule a tour, call (206) 632-5100 or visit www.theochocolate.com.

Hoist a Pint, or Two, or . . .
Redhook

Writing this entry was a labor of love—especially the research, which was extensive as well as exhaustive.

The Redhook Web site says they poured their first pint of Redhook in 1982. Paul Shipman and Gordon Bowker (Gordon also founded Starbucks Coffee), capitalizing on the fact that the Northwest was the draft beer–drinking capital of America, rented an old transmission shop and took their shot—and their barley and hops—at the American dream.

In 1983, after making some inroads in Seattle's local beer market with the introduction of its Ballard Bitter (now called Ballard Bitter IPA), the guys moved their operation from the 5,000-square-foot shop to the 26,000-square-foot historic Seattle Electric Railway building. This allowed the additional space to establish a brewpub, the Trolleyman.

Tan? Well, Not So Much

An out-of-towner encountering Seattle-ites may mistake their bronze patina for a suntan. However, here's the thing: It's meteorologically, perhaps even biologically, impossible for a Seattleite to tan—no, really. The change in pigment you may perceive is actually an effect of oxidation. In other words, Seattleites don't tan; they rust.

Some people might think these "tans" are a product of tanning booths, spray-on solutions, or, preferably, a sojourn to Maui. However, those people would be wrong. What's responsible for most of these pseudo-suntans is much more sinister.

Scientists have determined that the sun doesn't shine enough to allow Seattleites' skin to dry completely. This causes the accumulation of iron in the human body to collect on the epidermis (yes, skin), where it's subject to oxidation. Although metal oxidation usually results in the degradation of an object, Seattle oxidation results in a more attractive Seattleite.

In 1987 Redhook introduced its flagship beer, ESB (Extra Special Bitters), which became an instant favorite—including with yours truly. In 1988 Redhook, with the help of a German company, built a state-of-the-art brewery. When demand continued to increase, Redhook built two additional breweries. The one in Woodinville, about 20 miles northeast of Seattle, includes Forecasters brewpub. Some 3,000 miles east, the brewpub at the Portsmouth, New Hampshire, location is called the Cataqua Public House.

Due to Redhook's Woodinville location being so close to the Sammamish River Bike Trail and, incidentally, the Sammamish River, Jody and I dine at Forecasters often and have used almost every mode of transportation we can think of to get our butts to a Redhook brew: We drove in a car, rode on a motorcycle, in-line skated, pedaled our bikes, paddled our canoe—oh, and walked. There are also hitching posts for horses, and we once saw two helicopter pilots/deputy sheriffs land nearby and come in for lunch.

Redhook's first significant business location (3400 Phinney Avenue North, Seattle) now houses Theo's Chocolate Factory. The brewery's current Washington location is approximately 20 miles northeast of Seattle at 14300 Northeast 145th Street, Woodinville. For more information call (425) 483-3232 or visit www.redhook.com.

Best Lei in Seattle—Aloha!
Hawai'i General Store

This is one of the most enjoyable of the curiosities I found in Seattle. It was especially pleasant because I learned of it during a return flight from the island of Kauai in the great state of Hawaii. I suppose it would have been even more pleasant if we'd been on the way *to* the islands, but . . . a segment of Hawaiian Airlines' in-flight video magazine, *Hona Hou,* featured the Hawai'i General Store—yes, in Seattle!

Gail Stringer, the store's cheery owner, says a frequent response when she was attempting to raise start-up capital for her dream was, "A Hawaii store in Seattle? Why?" Perhaps the best answer is, "Why not?" Many Seattleites, transplants from the islands or not, have a special place in their hearts for the island state.

It's not all that unusual to find restaurants with exotic cuisines from far-flung locales, but to find a store that sells everything you're likely to find in a shop in its place of origin is quite unusual. But that's what you'll find just west of Interstate 5, mere blocks from the University of Washington campus.

★ ★

Rumor has it you can get the best lei in the
city at the Hawai'i General Store.

Gail started her business after realizing there were a significant
number of Hawaiians, and Hawaii lovers, living in Seattle unable to find
Hawaiian items locally, especially fresh leis. Gail is especially proud of
her leis, and with a devilish grin she quipped, "This is where you can
get the best lei in Seattle." Quibbling with such an assertion wouldn't
be polite.

You can even get the "delicacy" known as poi here. Poi is definitely
an acquired taste—one, I have to admit, I haven't acquired. Fresh poi
is available each Thursday. Perhaps adventurous Ballard-bound folks of
Scandinavian decent can pick up an order of poi on the way to their
next lutefisk feast.

★ ★

When Jody and I walked out of the Hawai'i General Store, we lamented not having applied a coat of SPF 30. We swore we actually got sunburned while shopping! Visiting this store is more fun than surfing Maui's famous Jaws—in a grass skirt!

Hawai'i General Store is located at 258 Northeast 45th Street. For more information call (206) 633-5233 or visit www.hawaiigeneral store.net.

Seattle's Favorite Drive-In Grub

Dick's Drive-In

Dick's Drive-In is Seattle's quintessential burger joint. If you're a Seattleite of any stripe hankerin' for a slab of beef wedged between two buns accompanied by a quiver of fries, there's no substitute.

Armed with an idea—and a duffle bag of perseverance—to open a drive-in rather than a sit-down burger restaurant, on January 28, 1954, Dick Spady, Warren Ghormley, and Dr. B. O. A. Thomas opened the first Dick's Drive-In in the Wallingford neighborhood. Their goal: serving fast, fresh, quality food at thin-wallet prices.

Although many "fast-food" joints were expanding nationally, Dick's preferred to remain a Seattle brand. It expanded only within the city, with four more restaurants: on Broadway in 1955; near Ballard in 1960; in Lake City in 1963; and the only sit-down Dick's, in lower Queen Anne, in 1974.

I can claim a connection to this Seattle icon. Dick's is so freakin' popular that they hire off-duty cops on weekends to help keep their customers safe. I worked the job for about three years.

My favorite story illustrates just how ingrained into Seattle culture—and diet—Dick's has become. A lady drove in just after closing time. She jumped out of her car and sprinted to the window, pleading for them to open.

We told her the restaurant had closed. She hesitated for a second then turned and breathed fire at us. "You don't understand," she began. "I live on Vashon Island. I can't get Dick's unless I come to

22,000 Acres of Lake

Lake Washington is King County's largest lake and the second largest in Washington, after Lake Chelan. Sparkling like a diamond, Lake Washington is 22 miles long and covers about 22,000 acres.

Lake Washington provides both commerce and recreation, at times combining the two. You'll find the Kenmore Air facility at the north end of the lake. You'll also find fishing, diving, sailing, boating, jet-skiing, canoeing, windsurfing, kite-boarding, and more. Scuba divers can find many adventures, too—the lake was home to a naval air station during WWII, and if you're lucky you may even find the wreckage of 1940s fighters.

There aren't many days when the temperatures rise into the 90s and 100s in Seattle, but Jody and I spent one of those days during summer 2007 on the lake. In those temperatures I can think of no better place to be than on the water. How we spent that day can give you an idea of what Lake Washington has to offer.

We explored the modest to opulent shoreline homes from north to south and baked in the sun as the few remaining skiers challenged the choppy waters. After sunbathing and satisfying our people-watching, it was time to satisfy our appetites. This is where Lake Washington shines. Neighborhood business centers along the lake, such as Madison Park and Leschi, are accessible via public docks. Just tie up and a short stroll later you'll be sitting at your choice of many of Seattle's best eateries.

One warning: The docks can be difficult to negotiate, especially if the water level is low and you have a ski boat. I swear, the last time I pulled into the Madison Beach tie-up, standing in my boat, the dock was at eye level.

Seattle. You people can get Dick's anytime you want." We apologized and told her that while we sympathized, there was nothing we could do. Then she said something that, for me, is forever tied to my experience at Dick's: "You cops are just 'Adam-Henrys'!" (Please, feel free to substitute a more accurate "A-H" phrase) "You're nice Adam-Henrys, but you're still Adam-Henrys!" She then drove off, hopefully to some burger rehab to suffer her Dick's Deluxe withdrawal—alone.

Also impressive is Dick's Drive-In's commitment to the basic work ethic and to its employees. Dick's only accepts payment in cash and requires its employees to make change the "old-fashioned" way, by adding and subtracting—in their heads. Dick's is also famous for its generosity to local charities, as well as for its employee student scholarship program.

Dick's Drive-In has locations at 111 Northeast 45th Street (Wallingford), 115 Broadway Avenue East, 9208 Holman Road NW (Ballard), 12325 30th Avenue North (Lake City), and 500 Queen Avenue North (Queen Anne). For more information call the corporate office at (206) 634-0300 or visit www.ddir.com.

A Garden of Special Note
Sound Garden

"IDs, please?" asked the security officer at the guard shack.

"Excuse me," I said, baffled at having to identify myself simply to gawk at a piece of outdoor artwork.

Not people to question authority, Jody and I cooperated and were allowed access. We crossed a footbridge, its surface and handrails embedded with crisscrossed poetic verse, and came into the presence of one of the most unique artworks in Seattle: the *Sound Garden*.

Approaching the site, we realized that had our eyes been closed or had it been the black of night, we still would have found what we'd come looking for: A ghostly melody emanated from the *Sound Garden*.

Check out this wind-whipped symphony. Its ghostly melodies will transport your spirit.

Created by artist Doug Hollis in 1983, the sculpture is located on National Oceanic and Atmospheric Administration (NOAA) property in Seattle's Sand Point neighborhood. The twelve towers composing the *Sound Garden* sit atop a knoll just north of the boundary separating NOAA property from Magnuson Park on the northwest shores of Lake Washington.

Security guards and the need to present ID are a result of heightened federal security since 9/11. You may photograph the *Sound Garden*—just remember to frame your shots so that you don't capture the NOAA facility in the background. The sparkling waves of Lake Washington and snowcapped peaks of the Cascade Mountains make a much better backdrop for your photos anyway.

Don't let the heightened security dissuade you from visiting this remarkable piece of art. On first inspection, you might be put off by the austere appearance of the dozen 20-foot gray steel towers reminiscent of derricks dotting an Oklahoma oil field. But you only have to close your eyes to receive the true gift Hollis has given Seattle— marvelous musical instruments played solely by the wind.

Each tower encases a long pipe organ–type cylinder that produces a unique tone. When the wind blows, a weathervane-type paddle mounted at the top of each tower swivels and generates sound through the tubes that then flows out into the world. Together they join in a surreal and unpredictable symphony. No two concerts are ever alike.

As for you fans of one of Seattle's most successful rock bands, Soundgarden, who might be wondering if this sculpture is where the group got its name—now you know.

Access to *Sound Garden* is through Magnuson Park, 7400 Sand Point Way Northeast.

Planes, Ahoy!
Sand Point Naval Air Station

Most folks are surprised to discover that a military airfield operated only a "stone's throw" from downtown Seattle for fifty years. The former airfield is now home to a National Oceanic and Atmospheric Administration (NOAA) station, a public art walk, and a popular city park.

Aside from visiting the *Sound Garden* sculpture, which anchors an interesting art walk, my connection to the former airbase is primarily the Magnuson Park boat ramps, where I routinely humiliate myself with my less-than-elegant seamanship skills.

The aptly named Sand Point NAS was located on a flat, sandy peninsula that juts out into Lake Washington on the eastern edge of the Sand Point neighborhood. Originally a joint Army-Navy facility, it eventually grew into a 400-acre naval air station, with a complement of more than 8,000 military and civilian personnel.

Seattle's Got Your Goats

Today you're the hero, tomorrow you're the "goat." However, even in Seattle, where more than a few Seahawks, Mariners, and Sonics have been the goat, being a goat in this town may not be such a bad thing. Just ask Snowflake and Brownie.

In Seattle's Madrona area, a hilly neighborhood that slopes to Lake Washington, a neighbor complained to the Department of Planning and Development about a zoning violation. "My neighbor is keeping smelly goats in the city," he reported.

With a due diligence rarely seen in matters of substance, never mind frivolity, the city found that the neighbor, Jennie Grant, did indeed share her property with two of the diminutive, bearded ruminants.

With atypical swiftness, the city "helped" the complaining neighbor by passing a city ordinance allowing residents to keep pygmy goats as pets. As for the neighbor whose—ironically—goat was got, he or she might do well to remember the adage: "I'm from the government and I'm here to help."

Originally outside Seattle's city limits, the area was occupied by several small farms, which King County purchased to facilitate the airbase. The first military flight to land at the base was flown by Major Henry K. Muhlenberg on October 8, 1921. He flew his biplane from (then) Camp Lewis and landed on a dirt runway.

Although many spectacular incidents have occurred at the airbase, including crash landings on land and in the lake, the most remarkable endeavor was probably a flight that occurred on April 7, 1924. On that date planes took off from Sand Point, which had been chosen as the beginning and ending airport for the first circumnavigation of the earth by air. After 26,345 miles the planes landed at Sand Point on September 28, 1924, to a cheering throng 50,000 strong.

After its heyday during WWII, the base's use declined, with the military deferring to bases in Puget Sound, particularly on Whidbey Island. Sand Point NAS ceased flight operations in 1970, but visitors can still explore remnants of paved runways and several structures from the original base.

The old air station is primarily located in and best accessed through Warren G. Magnuson Park at 7400 Sand Point Way NE. For more information on the history of the air station, visit www.historylink.org/index.cfm?DisplayPage=output.cfm&File_Id=2249.

2

West

The west area *of the city is anchored by Downtown, with Seattle Center and SoDo (South Downtown) serving, respectively, as its north and south bookends. Not to be confused with West Seattle, which is actually in southwest Seattle, this is the heart of Seattle. You could spend months here and still not see and do everything the area has to offer. Let's just take one day:*

Of course your first morning visit is to the Pike Place Market, where you grab a latté and a scone from the original Starbucks. You then wander the inscribed tiles of the market, watching as the vendors set up much as they did a century ago.

Now it's about noon; how about we stroll, cab, or bus it over to the Seattle Center? Hungry from all that walking at the market? Choose from a variety of restaurants in the Center House. Next let's check out the singing fountain and watch as streams of water shoot out to strains of Beethoven's "Ode to Joy" or some other classical ditty.

Now we're admiring McCaw Hall, home of the Pacific Northwest Ballet. From here we can gaze up at the Space Needle or west toward the Pacific Science Center. What to do next? Of course you have to ride to the top of the Needle, but perhaps you also should take in the exhibits at the Science Center or a movie at one of the two IMAX theaters. And you still haven't ridden the Smith Tower elevator, visited the waterfront, or strolled Chinatown—but hey, there's always tomorrow.

The Pedal Police
Seattle Police Mountain Bikes

This is another entry that strikes home with me. While I was never assigned to a full-time bike squad, I had the pleasure of riding police mountain bikes within my patrol squad for quite some time during the mid-1990s. I also accepted the illustrious position of East Precinct Mountain Bike coordinator, which roughly translates to the guy who fixes flats for other officers who were too lazy to fix their own.

Cops on bikes are not exactly new in America, but their initial heyday was in the late nineteenth century through the turn of the twentieth, before the automobile and motorcycle took over street duty. The modern incarnation of the police bicycle patrol began in Seattle in July 1987 when two Seattle police officers began riding mountain bikes on patrol. One of those officers was Paul Grady, and I was privileged to have him as my instructor when I participated in the Police Mountain Bike training program.

By 1991 there were a dozen officers working Downtown, silently slipping through the streets scaring the innards out of would-be bad guys attempting to commit would-be crimes. Criminals, used to keeping their heads on a swivel for the footsteps of beat officers or the stand-out-like-a-big-blue-sore-thumb patrol car, had little chance with the swift and silent bikes. The bike guys give miscreants fits as they swoosh from out of nowhere with their version of "Boo!"

If you spend any time in downtown Seattle, you'll likely see Mountain Bike Patrol officers zipping through traffic and riding up and down stairs—yes, they ride *up* stairs, too. If you see bike officers—who aren't busy crushing crime—go on over and say "Hi." They might even let you pet their bikes.

Like Rome, Seattle's Built on Seven Hills —or So

In 387 A.D. Saint Ambrose said, "When in Rome, do as the Romans do." Well, early Seattle land developers, in an effort to lure folks to the Northwest wilderness, drew a caparison between seven hills in Seattle and the seven hills of ancient Rome.

However, anyone who has traversed the Emerald City knows that there are more than seven significant hills across Seattle's undulating Vashon Glacier–carved landscape. One thing Seattle actually does have in common with Romulus's namesake city is that both cities have a Capitol Hill (Capitoline Collina).

Seattle's seven (or eight, or nine, or . . .) hills are Beacon (yes, for the one in Boston), West Seattle, Dearborn, Jackson, Second (Renton), First (Pill, Yesler, or Profanity), Capitol, Denny, Queen Anne (Temperance), and Magnolia Bluff. (Parentheses indicate previous names.)

To add to, or rather subtract from, the issue, Seattle actually flattened two of the hills: the Jackson Regrade south of Downtown and the more famous Denny Regrade to the north, which ironically brought the number of remaining hills to seven.

Dinner and a Movie
Big Picture

Elegant, exquisite, exceptional—how many "E" words can you come up with to describe Big Picture? Well, I suppose we could add a couple more—excellent and extraordinary—because they certainly fit, too.

Keep Clam, Your Majesty

Talk about a true Seattle character and you're probably talking about Ivar Haglund. The folksinger, who could reportedly sing more than 200 songs from memory, was alternately known as the King, Mayor, and/or Patriarch of the Seattle Waterfront. The half-Swedish, half-Norwegian born on March 20, 1905, was also a TV and radio personality, a property owner, and the founder of Ivar's Acres of Clams restaurant chain, whose slogan was to "Keep Clam!"

Ivar had a singular sense of humor and displayed that humor to his benefit, and perhaps his neighbor's detriment, at every turn. Ivar opened an aquarium at Pier 54 and soon after opened a fish-and-chips bar. I suppose if things didn't work out at the aquarium, the fish could remain of some value next door.

And speaking of next door, when Ivar's neighbor on a adjacent pier put up a sign admonishing folks not to feed the seagulls, Ivar—contrary as ever— put up his own sign, which read: SEAGULLS WELCOME. SEAGULL LOVERS WELCOME TO FEED SEAGULLS IN NEED.

In 1983, as a prank, Ivar tossed his captain's cap into the ring for a position as a port commissioner. Despite the gag candidacy, Ivar won the election by the considerable margin of 30,000 votes.

Okay, so I've set you up for spectacular, right? Let's say you're coming to Seattle to celebrate a loved one's birthday. You're staying in a hotel and they have a nice meeting hall for your festivities, but it's blah. You've seen these before: four walls, a floor, a ceiling, some

★ ★

tables and chairs—big deal. The folks at Big Picture have too much class to scoff at such mundane accommodations, so I'll do it for them. Ha! Ha! Ha!

Big Picture bills itself as a "boutique meeting and event facility." The amenities are second to none: uniquely furnished meeting rooms, a spectacular bar, gourmet catering, and—get ready—an intimate, and decadently comfortable, movie theater that shows first-run flicks in addition to the art films you might expect.

So if you have a party to plan, have a business meeting where you really need to kiss someone's butt, or simply have a hankering for a movie and a martini, Big Picture is the only place to do it—literally. If you don't trust me, how about companies that could afford to hold their events anywhere? Microsoft, Starbucks, Costco, and an exhaustive list of other Seattle and national companies count themselves as customers of Big Picture. And if those aren't good enough, the Foo Fighters, Will Smith, and Radiohead all held CD release parties at Big Picture.

Big Picture is located at 2505 First Avenue in downtown Seattle. For more information call (206) 256-0566 or visit www.thebigpicture.net.

Shrunken Heads, Mummies, and Stuff
Ye Olde Curiosity Shop

I was talking with a friend of mine from back East recently, and somehow we meandered onto the topic of shrunken heads. "You know, you just can't find a good shrunken head these days—and mummies, forget about it," my friend said.

"Oh, yeah," I replied. "Have I got a store for you."

A visit from family gave me the perfect opportunity to once again wander the shop. Although no one could ever see everything in the store in one visit, the shop simply is not open enough hours a day to accommodate that anyway. Each time you come back is like starting over. There's some really weird stuff here: novelties, Northwest native art, jewelry, and, yes, shrunken heads.

Any attempt to describe Ye Olde Curiosity Shop would be an injustice. Just go there already!
Courtesy Robert L. Harris

You'll find an interesting mix of old and new, tacky and tasteful, and bizarre and more bizarre. If there were ever a place where the phrase "You have to see it to believe it" truly fits , this is it.

Just go there already!

Ye Olde Curiosity Shop is located at 1001 Alaskan Way. For more information call (206) 682-5844 or visit www.yeoldecuriosityshop.com.

★ ★

Trivia

The dog toothbrush was first used in Seattle.

"What? I Can't Hear You!"
Qwest Field

Qwest Field is the home field of two top-tier professional sports teams: the National Football League's Seattle Seahawks and Major League Soccer's newest expansion team, the Seattle Sounders (although the Sounders have been a professional soccer team in Seattle in one incarnation or another since the early 1970s).

Players on opposing football teams despise this field because of the crowd noise. The noise isn't actually deafening. You can hear just fine—you just can't hear anything except the crowd.

In August 2008 my son Bryan participated in a "Punt, Pass & Pint" competition at Qwest Field. Approximately 500 people participated in the KJR Sport's Radio–sponsored event. In case you were wondering, the "pint" portion of the competition was a nod to the Redhook brew that flowed throughout the event. Fortunately Bryan kicked very early in the competition and won Seahawks season tickets for 2008.

Qwest Field has a 67,000-seat capacity, with sideline seats only 52 feet from the field of play and end-zone seats a mere 40 feet away. Seventy percent of the seats are covered. The field accommodates regulation sizes for the NFL and Fédération Internationale de Football Association, or FIFA (soccer's governing association).

Obviously, the most important event held in Qwest Field to date was on January 22, 2006, when the Seahawks won the National Football Conference (NFC) Championship game, defeating the Carolina Panthers 34–14 and propelling Seattle to Superbowl XL against the

Pittsburgh Steelers in Detroit. (That game is another story, and I'm still not ready to talk about it.)

Qwest Field is located at 800 Occidental Avenue South. For more information call (206) 381-7555 or visit www.qwestfield.com/.

World Champions of— Hockey?

While Seattle loves its West Coast Hockey Association team, the Thunderbirds, a Seattle hockey team with a stellar achievement often gets lost in the cobwebs of Seattle sports history. In 1917 the Seattle Metropolitans, of the Pacific Coast Hockey Association, summited hockey's Mount Olympus by defeating the National Hockey Association's Montreal Canadiens to win the coveted Stanley Cup.

Seattle has the distinction of being home to the first American team to win what has become the oldest trophy that can be won for a professional sporting event in North America. Seattle ended twenty-three years of Stanley Cup domination by the Canadians, since the cup's inception in the 1893–94 season. Another ten years would pass before another American team, the New York Rangers, would win the cup.

The Seattle Metropolitans laced up their blades a final time for the 1923–24 season, after which the team folded due to low attendance. And here's one more interesting tidbit for you: The Metropolitans won the regular season title in their last season—and did it with a losing record of 14–16.

★ ★

From Here Seattle Sprang, Sprung—Oh, Whatever
Pioneer Square

Many neighborhoods would like to be considered the heart and soul of Seattle, but only one section of the city can truly claim this honor: Pioneer Square. Although the first pioneers initially settled at Alki Point in West Seattle, what would become the downtown core of Seattle took off in Pioneer Square.

Talk about history. The colorful history of Seattle is not only everywhere you look but also beneath your feet—"Underground Seattle" lies a mere story or two beneath the sidewalk you're shuffling along.

Pioneer Square encompasses roughly 20 city blocks featuring the most historic buildings of competing Victorian and Romanesque architecture in America. You'll also find more than 200 retail shops and eateries where you can fill your bellies and empty your wallets.

One feature that captivated me the moment I arrived in Seattle is the pergola, which sits in Pioneer Square Park. This glass-and-steel structure, which looks like an ornate, oversize bus shelter, was originally just that. It was erected in 1905 as a cable-car shelter for those waiting to ride up Yesler Way.

Among other features in the square, you can find the secluded Waterfall Garden at Second Avenue and Main Street. (This also marks the birthplace of the United Parcel Service, UPS.) Then there's Occidental Park, the Fallen Firefighters Memorial, and Klondike Gold Rush National Park (considered the nation's smallest national park); and let's not forget Underground Seattle at Doc Maynard's.

Pioneer Square hosts such events as the annual Mardi Gras celebration and Pioneer Square's Fire Festival. You can also participate in the First Thursday Gallery Walk. Meet other like-minded folks at 6:00 a.m. on the first Thursday of the month at Occidental Park, Occidental Avenue and Main Street. Then you're off for a casual stroll to many of Seattle's best art galleries.

Pioneer Square is located in South Downtown. For more information visit www.pioneersquare.org.

An Opium Den on Wheels?

The United Parcel Service (UPS) was born in Seattle with its initial, primarily mission to deliver opium (legal at the time). Most people are surprised at this—not just because of the opium thing but because, unlike Starbucks or Microsoft, the giant company no longer operates out of the Seattle area. In fact, UPS relocated to New York back in 1930, from there to Connecticut, and later to Atlanta, Georgia, where it's headquartered today.

James E. "Jim" Casey founded the company in 1907 as the American Messenger Company. In 1913 he merged with another small competitor and used the name Merchant's Parcel Delivery. Finally, in 1919 the company became the United Parcel Service, and it stuck.

At only nineteen years old, Jim started the company with a hundred borrowed bucks and a fleet of six bicycles. The fleet grew to include a motorcycle and a Model T Ford, and by 1915 there were five motorcycles and four cars. Today UPS has 88,000 ground vehicles and 300 aircraft painted in the ubiquitous brown hue, which was originally chosen to emulate the elegant Pullman railroad cars of the past. Jim served as CEO until retiring in 1962. UPS is now the largest parcel delivery company in America, employing more than 475,000 employees, with annual revenues of $47.5 billion.

Interested in reducing fuel consumption, UPS designed a computer program that maps out delivery routes that favor right turns at intersections (a pet peeve of mine), reducing idling time as well as, I would imagine, collision rates.

Probably the most interesting "package" UPS has ever delivered was one containing two whale sharks being transported from Taiwan to the Georgia Aquarium in Atlanta. UPS was the first delivery company to resume operations in Oklahoma City following the bombing and in New York City after 9/11. UPS celebrated its centennial on August 28, 2007.

A Wedge of Seattle History
The Sinking Ship Garage

At Second Avenue and Skid Road (aka Yesler Way), you'll find a pizza wedge–shaped slice of land and upon it one of the city's most interesting buildings. The Sinking Ship Garage is so named for obvious reasons. It looks like a ship sinking stern first, with only the bow yet to succumb to asphalt and concrete "waves."

This triangular parking garage appears as though it's a ship sinking stern first into the asphalt of Pioneer Square.

It's an eyesore to some and a historic "place keeper" to others who still regret the demolition of the Seattle Hotel, which stood here until 1961. From the air it looks as though the city has placed an arrow pointing out Pioneer Square to SeaTac-bound air passengers.

The garage survived plans for destruction after the state supreme court ruled the city could claim the land through eminent domain and demolish the hotel to make room for an extended monorail line. The monorail debacle is what they call a whole 'nother story. However, it did give the Sinking Ship Garage new life.

Perhaps the city will buy it for nostalgic reasons and government offices will return to Pioneer Square. I can see it now: the City of Seattle, Sinking Ship City Hall.

The Sinking Ship Garage is located at Second Avenue and Yesler Way.

Looking for a Good Sail?
Center for Wooden Boats

It isn't a surprise to find such a facility in a city known for its maritime culture. Even the Denny Party, Seattle's first non-Indian residents, arrived not by wagon but by boat, landing on Alki's shores. As with so many Seattle museums, the Center for Wooden Boats emphasizes a hands-on experience. If you've ever wondered how boats were made before fiberglass came along, get your landlubbing hands down to the center and build some history.

Master craftsmen will help you splice a line, caulk a seam, or steam-bend oak for a boat frame. You'll come away with not only a better understanding of how boats were built a century ago but also an appreciation of the skills necessary to produce such beautiful vessels.

If you want to take your experience beyond the shipwright's craft, you can participate in the sailor's craft and row, paddle, or set sail on the sparkling waves of Lake Union. Although every visit is special, you might want to plan a trip during the annual Lake Union Wooden Boat Festival.

The facility houses a boat livery where you can rent a boat for a sunny afternoon or summer evening sail on Lake Union and enjoy one of the most spectacular views of the Seattle skyline. Here's a tip: If you come on a Sunday afternoon, you can row or sail for free.

The Center for Wooden Boats is located at 1010 Valley Street. For more information call (206) 382-2628 or visit www.cwb.org.

★ ★

For landlubbers who want to experience a piece of Seattle's maritime history, there's no place better to do it than Seattle's Center for Wooden Boats. Sealubbers are welcome, too.

Many Happy Returns
Nordstrom

Although I'm not a big shopper—well, not for clothes and other such notions anyway—I thought it appropriate to give Nordstrom the attention it deserves as Seattle's quintessential shopping experience.

Nordstrom has a legendary national reputation for customer service, which is certainly a curiosity in today's world. If you have a problem with a purchase at "Nordy's," bringing it back for an exchange or refund will not have you feeling the least bit uncomfortable—they'll take care of you. In fact, a book about Nordstrom's customer service is now an industry (any industry) standard.

Mother (Madame) Damnable

Mary Ann Conklin's expletive expertise garnered her the moniker of Mother Damnable. People said she was caustically versed in many languages, but despite her invective fluency, she became the proprietor of Seattle's first hotel, the Felker House. She was encouraged by that semi-sophisticate, quasi-ruffian Doc Maynard, who had sold land for the hotel to Captain Leonard Felker. Doc felt a brothel was essential for attracting sailors, lumbermen—and their money—to Seattle.

Mother Damnable took pride in her hotel for its fresh linen, fine repast, and budding brothel upstairs. She rented out unused rooms for various purposes, not the least of which was the territorial court. (A court of law downstairs and brothel upstairs—strange bedfellows indeed.)

Mother Damnable died in 1873 and was buried in the Seattle Cemetery. When the city decided to replace the cemetery with Denny Park, her remains were moved to Lake View Cemetery. Legend says that when they dug her up, the coffin was inordinately heavy. Upon opening the lid, they found her remains had turned to stone.

Speaking of stones: On Mother's gravestone is inscribed DIED 1887, which is strange because that year's not only fourteen years after she died but also three years after they moved her grave.

Nordstrom's service was hilariously spoofed on Seattle's premier sketch comedy show, KING 5 TV's *Almost Live.* A man at the customer service counter has a problem. He informs the syrupy-sweet and overly

★ ★

polite customer service representative that he has to make a return. She of course says it will be no problem and asks for the item. The man places a partially eaten hamburger on the counter. The Nordstrom's clerk happily collects the burger in exchange for a full refund.

Now I'm not saying you should "return" your half-eaten Dick's Deluxe burger to Nordy's customer service counter, but you get the idea. I may not be a fashion plate myself, but I admire good service in any industry—and if the worst thing folks can do is parody how good you are, that's saying something.

Nordstrom is located at 500 Pine Street. For more information call (206) 448-8522 or visit http://shop.nordstrom.com.

It's a Museum, It's a Park—It's Both!
Olympic Sculpture Park

From their original building in Volunteer Park (now the Asian Art Museum), to the ever-expanding downtown flagship location, and now to Olympic Sculpture Park—its newest and most curious facility—the Z-shaped museum/park, located adjacent to Myrtle Edwards Park along Puget Sound, aims to impress and hits the mark.

The view of Puget Sound alone makes the park/museum worth the trip, but there's so much more. I'll begin with one I'm a tad fond of: *Eagle,* by sculptor Alexander Calder, previously sat on the lawn of the Asian Art Museum in Volunteer Park, which has been within my police beat for many years. Semi-ignorant art aficionado that I am, I'd always thought the vivid orange conglomeration was a leaping orca (killer whale). Apparently, it's an eagle—my bad.

This park, built on the site of an old oil facility, has a truly fascinating and multiple-award-winning design. Constructed in a Z shape, the museum sits across the street from the Old Spaghetti Factory at 2901 Western Avenue. The park zigs over the roadway and then zags back over the train tracks. The bottom of the Z catches the lapping waves of Puget Sound.

Olympic Sculpture Park offers art by the sea—oh, and by the park, and by the street, and by the railroad tracks, and by the . . .

The zigzag shape is striking in that, along with the unique sculptures, it allows visitors to gain varied perspectives from within a relatively small space. You can easily access the museum, opened on January 20, 2007, by heading west on Broad Street from the Space Needle. Stop before you get wet, and voila!

Olympic Sculpture Park is located at 2901 Western Avenue. For more information call (206) 654-3100 or visit http://seattleartmuseum .org/visit/OSP/default.asp#tours.

✦ ✦

Sorry, Honey, I Forgot to Geoduck!

The word *geoduck* (GOO-eee-duck) comes from a Lushootseed (Puget Sound Salishan Indian language) word meaning "dig deep." It is the only Lushootseed word to have made it into the English language.

In keeping with its name, the geoduck secrets itself within thick mud under deep water. What does it look like? Hmmm. Well, the geoduck is basically a massively huge and infinitely ugly clam. It has a 6- to 8-inch-diameter shell, but the resemblance to any ordinary clam ends there. A geoduck's body can extend out of the shell up to 4 feet, with a diameter of 2 inches.

However, I'm warning you: Please don't go shopping for one of these with your Grandma. A polite observer might compare the protuberance to an elephant's trunk; I'm apparently not that refined. With my junior high sense of propriety, noticing the geoduck's resemblance to a certain part of the male anatomy is unavoidable. In fact, the sight can be so striking, I'd venture it might have caused Seattle's own Gypsy Rose Lee to blush.

Something Fishy Here
Seattle Aquarium

As a scuba diver, I love the Seattle Aquarium. Viewing marine life in this aquarium on Pier 59 is the next best thing to diving among them.

Since its opening in 1977, the Seattle Aquarium, operated by the Seattle Department of Parks and Recreation, has hosted more than

★ ★

nineteen million visitors. In 2007 it broke attendance records with an astonishing 811,000 guests.

On June 22, 2007, the aquarium reopened following a $41.5-million expansion project. Along with a face-lift of the main entrance hall, the gift shop was expanded to more than 2,600 square feet. A 140-seat cafe was added, which can be rented for special events. The new Window on Washington Waters and the Crashing Waves exhibits will thrill visitors young, old, and betwixt.

The Seattle Aquarium focuses on Washington State waters, with exhibits such as the previously mentioned Window on Washington Waters presenting salmon and other native marine life swimming among the sea anemones and undulating kelp. What makes this exhibit curious is that rather than having a landlubber delivering dry facts about the tank's denizens, divers enter the tank three times a day wearing special diving masks that allow them to answer questions from onlookers on the dry side of the tank.

Other exhibits include marine life in tidepools, coral reefs, odd creatures, seabirds, and marine mammals. The aquarium boasts a large underwater dome that provides visitors with a bottom-up, rather than a side or top-down, perspective on Puget Sound marine life. Similar to the Window on Washington Waters exhibit, a diver answers questions daily when he enters the tank at 1:30 p.m. to feed the fish.

Currently, Leonard the Goldfish is preoccupied with getting himself into the aquarium. Leonard even has his own Myspace.com Web site and a Youtube.com video where he discusses his plight with sympathetic harbor seals. I support Leonard's efforts, and by the time you read this, he may very well have found a home. However, considering the size of some of the current residents—not to mention the saline content of the water—I would caution ol' freshwater Leonard to be careful what he wishes for. He may just get it.

The Seattle Aquarium is located at 1483 Alaskan Way. Hours are 9:30 a.m. to 5:00 p.m. daily (last entry at 5:00 p.m.), 9:30 to 3:00 p.m. on Thanksgiving and Christmas Eve, and noon to 5:00 p.m. Christmas

Day. For more information call (206) 386-4300 or visit www
.seattleaquarium.org.

Get the Picture?
Art Walk

The Seattle Art Walk is not for the weak of spirit, or the weak of leg. If
you want to spend any time in each of the many galleries, you're probably going to have to divide this cultural adventure into several days.

With twenty galleries spread out over some 16 downtown city
blocks, you might have to hire a personal trainer before attempting the
event—as with walking almost anywhere in downtown Seattle, hills
are involved. This may prompt the exclamation, as my inappropriately
shod mother once observed during a visit, "This is not awesome!"
However, this is a temporary condition that immediately reverses once
you're inside a gallery, soaking up the myriad works to be gawked at,
considered, and perhaps purchased.

And you'll certainly have no worries about sustenance during your
trek. Many fine eateries are interspersed among the gallery locations,
including eighteen of the very best restaurants Seattle has to offer.
These are listed on the Art Walk map (information provided below).

For those of you who may not need repast but desire a bit of
hydration after tramping such a distance, one of the galleries on First
Avenue boasts a wine bar. (Perhaps that's why it's an art walk, not an
art drive.)

There's no single address for the walk, so your best bet is to go to
http://seattleartwalk.org for a detailed map of the Art Walk and for
more information.

A Whole New Meaning for Park & Ride
Freeway Park

Superman's Fortress of Solitude—that's what Seattle's unique city
park that straddles Interstate 5 through Downtown brings to mind.

Freeway Park is actually built over a major interstate. You can picnic on a soft grassy patch as hundreds of cars pass.

Freeway Park is a concrete labyrinth of severe geometric forms piercing into and jutting out of the emerald green that blankets the park and whose shadows change its appearance by the moment. And a measure of metropolitan solitude is exactly what this phantasmagorical park provides people passing through or settling in for a picnic lunch on a warm, sunny afternoon before returning to work in one of the myriad surrounding high-rise office buildings.

I've long enjoyed and admired this place, where a bustling metropolis and a serene park floating above a freeway meet in a harmonic collision. The 5.2-acre park, dedicated on July 4, 1976, was built upon a lid that caps I-5 where the freeway dips as it skirts the eastern edge of downtown Seattle at the western base of First Hill. Freeway Park was the first park of its kind—built over a freeway running through a major metropolitan area—in the United States.

Enjoy a stroll through this inviting park. The lighting has been enhanced, and the convention center that adjoins the park has increased video surveillance and security bicycle patrols, helping park guests feel safe.

The L-shaped park is located at 700 Seneca Street, roughly between Seneca Street to the south, University Street to the north, Sixth Avenue to the west, and Hubble Place to the east. For more information contact Seattle Parks and Recreation at (206) 684-4075 or visit www .seattle.gov/parks/park_detail.asp?ID=312.

This Is So Beneath You
Seattle Underground

No book about Seattle curiosities would be complete without mentioning Seattle's underground. When you visit Seattle, take Bill Speidel's Underground Tour! If you were born in Seattle and haven't done it yet, take this tour! Why am I so emphatic about this? I'd been living in Seattle for almost twenty years before I finally checked out these suburban catacombs.

The adventure begins with tour guides who could moonlight in Seattle's comedy clubs. They skillfully put visitors in the mood to explore Seattle's literal underbelly. From early Seattle history to poking fun at Tacoma, it's a party atmosphere as you leave the bright, "modern" environs of Doc Maynard's Pub and descend into a dim, dank, and sometimes delightfully decadent history.

On June 6, 1889, the Great Seattle Fire took much of Downtown to the ground. When rebuilding the damaged section of the city,

A City of Book-worms

Seattle is considered one of the most literate cities in the country. A survey at Central Connecticut State University, titled "America's Most Literate Cities," named Seattle #1 twice, in 2005 and 2006, and #2 in 2004 and 2007, seesawing with Minneapolis, and finally tying with Minneapolis for the honor in 2008. The study is based on a number of literate behaviors (reading-type stuff), such as the number of bookstores and libraries, newspaper circulation, educational levels achieved, literacy rates, and publishing successes.

This was one of the first factoids people told me about Seattle when I first arrived. Folks in New York, Chicago, Los Angeles, and, to a lesser degree, Boston and Philadelphia just assume you know everything about their cities that's worth knowing. However, Seattleites seem to find it a cultural mandate to inform you of every miniscule morsel of trivia about Seattle's being biggest, best, first, oldest, richest, deepest, loudest, softest, highest, fastest, etc. For me, I like living in a literate city. You read me?

planners decided to raise the city's elevation one to two stories above the original grade. Early Seattle settlers had originally built Seattle on often-flooding tidelands. Somehow they hadn't noticed the difference in moisture content between the high and low tides. The fire gave Seattle a chance for a civil engineering do-over, or what golfers might call a massive, metropolitan mulligan.

Some sidewalks remained up to 36 feet below the new grade, forcing folks to brave ladders to access some shops. Eventually the old sidewalks were covered and new ones raised to the new entrances. For those stores that survived the fire and whose entrances remained at the original level—now underground—glass cubes, similar to small glass bricks, were embedded in the sidewalk, allowing natural light into the subterranean mercantiles. Some of this glass, which the sun's rays have turned a translucent violet, remain to this day.

The underground was condemned in 1907 due to safety and bubonic plague concerns, but illegal gambling houses, brothels, flop-houses, speakeasies, and opium dens remained for many years. The tour covers only a portion of Seattle's underground, but you'll certainly get the idea.

It's a good idea to call before you visit; some days the tours can get crowded.

Bill Speidel's Underground Tour is located at 608 First Avenue. For more information call (206) 682-4646 or visit http://undergroundtour .com.

Once the Tallest
Smith Tower

It's hard to believe that in a country as big and growing as the early twentieth-century United States, with expanding metropolises such as Boston, Chicago, and Los Angeles, that it was then teensy-weensy— but very rugged—Seattle that actually boasted the tallest skyscraper in the country outside Manhattan, and the fourth-tallest building in the world. In fact, at 522 feet, Seattle's Smith Tower reigned (no pun intended) as the tallest building west of the Mississippi River until 1962, when a new crosstown upstart, the Space Needle, shot about 40 feet higher into Seattle's gray skies.

Lyman Cornelius Smith, East Coast gun maker (the Ithaca Gun Company, not Smith & Wesson) and founder of the Smith Corona Typewriter Company, began building the tower in 1910, but the poor fellow died before its completion.

No longer the tallest skyscraper west of Ohio, Smith Tower is still the oldest and as handsome as ever.

One jewel of the Smith Tower is the exotically appointed Chinese Room, located on the thirty-fifth floor. One facet of this jewel is the Wishing Chair. A legend holds that if a willing single woman sits in the chair, she will marry within a year. Hogwash you say? Well, don't say that too loud—Lyman Smith's ghost might return to haunt you. His very own daughter married within a year of plunking her posterior on that plushy seat.

This historic and pioneering skyscraper has many unique characteristics. The first two floors of the exterior are clad in granite, but the remainder wears terra-cotta. Of its seven Otis elevators (still run by human operators), six function with their original DC motors. And get this: Most of the 2,314 windows contain their original 1914 glass. At its pinnacle once perched a 10,000-gallon water tower and a small caretaker's apartment. After dissembling the cast-iron tower and cutting it into pieces small enough to fit into the elevators, building owners replaced the void with a three-story penthouse. It is currently the only dwelling in Smith Tower, and the residents have an incredible view of Mount Rainier—if it's not overcast, that is.

Smith Tower is located at 506 Second Avenue. For more information visit www.smithtower.com.

This One's a Classic
The Seattle Symphony

Although I tend toward the head-banging end of the music radio dial, I believe that a symphony orchestra is essential to a city's cultural personality.

The Seattle Symphony has distinguished itself in many ways. First, for such a relatively young American city, the Seattle Symphony's history stretches back more than a century to its first performance on December 29, 1903. Conducted by Gerard Schwartz since 1983, the symphony boasts more than 36,000 subscribed patrons; conducts well over 200 performances per year, attracting an annual audience of 315,000; and has toured Europe. Innovative and prolific, the symphony has made more than one hundred recordings and has garnered eleven Grammy nominations.

In 2001 the symphony started the Soundbridge Seattle Symphony Music Discovery Center. Through classes, exhibits, and musical performances, the center has introduced classical music to almost 90,000 persons, most notably students from 190 regional schools.

It seems the symphony is not satisfied with vying for Grammy Awards within its presumed genre. In 2006 the orchestra received an Emmy Award for its television special, "Seattle Symphony from Benaroya Hall."

The Seattle Symphony is located at Benaroya Hall, 200 University Street. For more information call (206) 215-4700 or visit www.seattle symphony.org.

Seattle's Summer Bash

Seafair

Seafair is Seattle's preeminent annual celebration, offering Seattleites everything from a milk carton derby to neighborhood parades, the Thunderboats on Lake Washington, and the festival's highlight, the sky-ripping performance by the U.S. Navy Blue Angels. Seafair's roots actually began during the early planning stages for Seattle's centennial in 1951. However, organizers couldn't wait—the first Seafair event, the Seafair Grande Parade (later Torchlight Parade), was held in August 1950. Seafair events were designed to emphasize marine activities in line with Seattle's reputation as a world-renowned maritime capital.

The City of Seattle, the U.S. Coast Guard, and the U.S. Navy developed a close relationship planning Seafair; a bond that continues to this day. The Navy and Coast Guard schedule Seattle port calls for ships during the height of Seafair activities in late July to early August. Ships from the Canadian Navy also make port calls during Seafair.

Some two million folks enjoy at least one Seafair event each year. Of course during summer, you can't swing a dead hydroplane without hitting a Seafair-sanctioned event. Events have featured some of the most popular celebrities in the world, including Bob Hope, JFK, Tim Conway, Ernest Borgnine, Ted Turner, and Washington State's own Bing Crosby.

Even Seattle's suburbs get into the act. For example, Mountlake Terrace holds its own Seafair-sanctioned Tour de Terrace. And well

★ ★

after the last rooster tails have subsided on the lake, another Seafair event, the Seafair & 76 Special People's Holiday Cruise, takes place in December.

For more information on Seafair, write to 2200 Sixth Avenue, Suite 400, Seattle 98121; call (206) 728-0123; or visit www.seafair.com.

Trivia

The world's first hydroplane racing boat was built in Seattle.

Turn Off the Lights, the Party's—Starting
Torchlight Parade

Since August 12, 1950, the City of Seattle has held what has become the preeminent parade during Seattle's midsummer Seafair celebration. In its first year the parade was known as the Seafair Grande Parade and was held during the day in downtown Seattle.

Now held at night, the Torchlight Parade begins in the early evening and marches into dusk. By the time the last float has glided past the grandstand, darkness has blanketed the parade route except for speckles of light from a plethora of personal illumination devices.

The parade route has changed over the years but has always coursed through portions of Downtown. The current route has marchers snaking their way from the Space Needle at Seattle Center south to Qwest Field, home of the Seattle Seahawks and Seattle Sounders.

The Torchlight Parade features an eclectic mix of participants, including the quintessential Seafair Pirates. Arrrgh, Matey! The Pirates are joined by the Seafair Clowns, Dragon Dancers, and several hydroplanes and their drivers. Crisply uniformed soldiers, sailors, marines, and airmen from nearby military bases also march proudly. Add the Seattle Seahawks Cheerleaders, the University of Washington and local high school marching bands, politicians, and other civic leaders and you've got yourself a parade unlike any you've ever seen.

There's something very American about a parade. However, the Torchlight Parade, while certainly no less American, is very much a Seattle parade—from a city that's never been big on doing things the way everyone else does them.

Trivia

The gas turbine *Victoria Clipper IV* catamaran that shuttles between Seattle and Victoria, British Columbia, is the fastest passenger vessel in the western hemisphere.

No, Not like Tinkerbell
Washington State Ferries

The Washington State Ferry system, which pitches and catches ferries from its busiest port on the Seattle waterfront, is the largest ferry system in the United States. Its twenty-eight vessels serve eight Washington counties and one Canadian province, British Columbia, along ten routes from twenty terminals.

These are indeed impressive facts, but my admiration, bordering on affection, for the ferry system comes from one of my favorite recreations: riding the ferry for pleasure. If I just made ferry commuters who suffer long lines, delays, crashes, and other ferry system mishaps on a regular basis wince, forgive me. I'm coming from a purely pleasure-seeking perspective.

Washington State ferries serve several communities in Washington and British Columbia.

There's something immensely enjoyable about a leisurely ferryboat ride across Puget Sound, especially if you walk on and don't have to worry about the mad car scramble, like bees to and from a hive. Hop a ferry on a fine afternoon and cruise over to Vashon Island, Whidbey Island, or the Kitsap Peninsula for a warm bowl of soup in winter or a cold pint of your favorite microbrew in summer.

And speaking of summer, here's a cool tip for motorcyclists: On ferries, motorcycles are treated to first-on, first-off status. And get this—they'll even charge you less for the privilege. So get your motor runnin' . . .

For more information on the Washington State Ferry System, call (206) 515-3400 or visit www.wsdot.wa.gov/ferries.

Get Your Motor Runnin'

This is a special one for me, as I'm a motorcycle aficionado—to say the least. I've belonged to a police-firefighter motorcycle club for years and commute to work daily on my Harley-Davidson. Another reason this entry is special is that one of the Seattle Cossacks, the legendary Dave Eady—a lifetime member of the group, a friendly giant of a man, and an uncannily skilled rider—is a personal friend of mine.

The Seattle Cossacks are a motorcycle stunt-riding team that have been thrilling crowds for more than sixty years, with only a short break to fight a little skirmish called World War II. The members, from the oldest (age seventy-four) to the youngest (in his twenties), ride classic Harley-Davidsons manufactured between 1930 and 1949.

The group came together to promote the positive aspects of motorcycling, and I don't know anyone who has done the motorcycling world more of a service in this endeavor. I've seen the Cossacks perform at numerous events around the Northwest, and each time I'm as amazed as I was the previous time. These guys are the real deal—no fancy "Hollywood" trappings or production values, just barebones, seat-of-their-pants riding of real motorcycles. Rain or shine, these bikers aim to please and hit the bull's-eye every single time.

I dare you to come away from one of their thirty or so shows a year unimpressed with just how many men can ride on one motorcycle. And I'm talking about men of from lean to, how shall I put it, significant proportions. One after another, they pile high and then flare out low—faces mere inches from the asphalt—riding so close to the crowd that spectators can't help but feel a part of the show.

For more information visit www.seattlecossacks.com.

★ ★

A Streetcar Named—Undesirable

South Lake Union Streetcar

The city of Seattle has a long and checkered streetcar history, from the Seattle-Everett Interurban Line of the early twentieth century to the George Benson Waterfront Streetcar Line that runs along, yep, you guessed it, the waterfront.

The South Lake Union Streetcar is a fun way to explore the city—in purple or orange.

In December 2007 Seattle added to its trolley transit tradition with the now-named South Lake Union Streetcar. However, locals originally used the word "trolley" instead of "streetcar." Astute readers have just perked up. Some shrewd capitalists at the Kapow! Coffee Shop certainly did.

Capitalizing on the acronym for the trolley line's local name (some say the original official name), the South Lake Union Trolley, a barista for the shop created T-shirts inviting people to "Ride the SLUT." Initial orders sold out in a blink, with lines out the door and huge reorders.

The SLUT runs about 2.5 miles, connecting the restaurant and marina areas of South Lake Union with the Westlake Mall. The route also allows folks the opportunity to easily transfer to other forms of city transportation, including the Seattle Center Monorail.

So enjoy an old-fashioned streetcar ride, and don't forget the new motto: "Ride the SLUS." Doesn't have the same punch, does it?

The South Lake Union Streetcar runs between Westlake Mall and South Lake Union. For more information call (206) 553-3000 or visit www.seattlestreetcar.org.

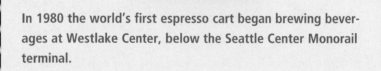

Trivia

In 1980 the world's first espresso cart began brewing beverages at Westlake Center, below the Seattle Center Monorail terminal.

Watch Out for Flying Fish
Pike Place Public Market

If you find yourself in downtown Seattle at the cobblestone intersection of Pike Street and Pike Place and see fish flying by, a 600-pound piggybank, and a brown Starbucks coffeeshop sign, you haven't just followed Alice through the looking glass. You're actually standing in the middle of Seattle's most popular tourist attraction—the Pike Place Public Market, or simply, The Market. This sprawling hundred-year-old, nine-acre facility, America's oldest continually operating farmers' market, draws some ten million people annually. Today it features more than 200 stores and hundreds of craft and farm produce stalls, but it wasn't always so imposing.

If you're in the market for a market, Pike Place
Public Market is the oldest in America.

Following incidents of price gouging by middlemen (onions in
particular went from 10 cents to a dollar a pound), a farmers' market
was established in August 1907. Some eight or so farmers transported
wagonloads of farm-fresh produce to a pier below the area where Pike
Place Public Market stands today. The size of the crowd on that very
first day rivaled that of an average day today—around 10,000 persons.

Over the years The Market has had its ups and downs. After the
attack on Pearl Harbor, Japanese-Americans, who operated two-thirds
of the booths at that time, were forced to relocate to internment
camps. The Market was nearly sold in the 1960s but instead became
public and was renovated. Now on the National Register of Historic
Places, it is secure as a public market.

As with many other curiosities in this book, my best recollections of The Market are personal. A childhood friend of mine had also moved to Seattle and especially loved The Market. When I returned to New England, Howard remained in Seattle and became a Market regular. Whenever I returned to Seattle, I simply strolled along The Market's inscribed tiles and never failed to find him. Another option was to listen for the street musicians, many of whom are quite talented. Howard, however, wasn't attracted by this category—bad blues guitar often signaled my friend's section of the sidewalk stage.

Pike Place Public Market is located at Pike Street and Pike Place. For more information visit www.pikeplacemarket.org.

This Little Piggy Went to (The) Market
Rachel the Pig

If you've ever been to the Pike Place Market, which is perennially among Seattle's most visited attractions, you've probably noticed *Rachel the Pig.* In fact, you may have even stumbled over or banged a knee into her if you weren't paying attention while flowing obliviously among the throng at the entrance beneath the famous public market center sign at Pike Street and Pike Place.

Rachel the Pig, installed at the marketplace in 1986, is a nearly 600-pound bronze pig cast in the image of the real Rachel—a 1977 Island County champion swine and Whidbey Island sculptor Georgia Gerba's neighbor and inspiration.

Rachel serves double duty as both a popular market mascot and, at the risk of typecasting her, a piggybank. That's right, Rachel is also a bona-fide piggybank. Folks from all over the globe deposit their change into her. The coins from many nations, amounting to about $9,000 annually, are donated to charity.

According to legend, rubbing Rachel's snout will bring you good luck.

Rachel the Pig is located in Pike Place Public Market at Pike Street and Pike Place.

★ ★

That little piggy may have gone home, but this little piggy went to market—and stayed. Bryan Pomper

So, You Want Moore?

The Moore Theater

The Moore Theater, the oldest theater in Seattle, turned one hundred years old in 2007. The venerable showplace is named for its original owner, James A. Moore, who was a force to be reckoned with during the famous Denny Regrade of downtown Seattle. One of the most beautifully constructed and equipped theaters in America, the Moore was the first structure to be built on the newly graded Second Avenue at Virginia Street, establishing the area as Seattle's theater district.

The theater's history is that of entertainment in America. For example, the Moore hosted an audience of 2,500 patrons for its inaugural performance, a comic opera called *The Alaskan,* which earned itself a trip to a successful run on Broadway in New York.

You know those time-lapse images of clouds passing or seasons changing? Well, it would be more than cool to see a time-lapse film of the Moore throughout the years. Can you imagine? Beginning with a comic opera that morphs into the Orpheum vaudeville circuit, which then blends into the Negro Ensemble, fading into opera singers and then a Kabuki troop. Next, boxing matches transform into the first home of the Seattle Film Festival and, later still, grunge-rock concerts.

However, some of you are probably more familiar with the Moore than you might think. Back in the early 1990s, MTV featured a video for the song "Even Flow" by iconic Seattle band Pearl Jam. The video comprised film footage shot during a concert held at the Moore Theater in January 1992. This compelling video, aside from being a great musical performance, shows off how the architecture combines a unique blend of classic Italian and Byzantine terra-cotta-styled venue with the modern mosh pit into which Eddie Vedder plops from an ornate theater balcony.

The Moore Theater is located at 911 Pine Street. For more information call (206) 467-5510 or visit www.themoore.com.

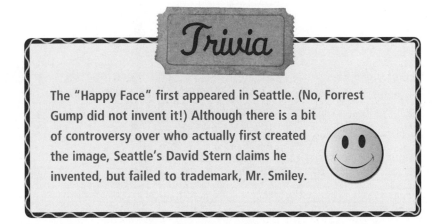

Trivia

The "Happy Face" first appeared in Seattle. (No, Forrest Gump did not invent it!) Although there is a bit of controversy over who actually first created the image, Seattle's David Stern claims he invented, but failed to trademark, Mr. Smiley.

★ ★

A Different Story
Bank of America Tower

The Bank of America Tower (BOAT), originally the Columbia Tower, soars above all other buildings in Seattle's skyline and, at seventy-six stories, is the building with the most number of floors on the West Coast. My wife, Jody, a professional firefighter, became intimately familiar with nearly every inch of this skyscraper's 997 feet while participating in the annual Firefighter Stair Climb charity event. Over a thousand firefighters from 200 departments climbed the 1,311 steps, raising $365,000 for the Leukemia & Lymphoma Society in 2007.

Can a skyscraper have more floors than any other on the West Coast but not be the tallest? You're looking at it.

I find skyscrapers interesting, but I'll admit that some, while impressively tall, are also boring. The BOAT is not one of these. From a distance its imposing black silhouette may appear strictly angular, but a closer inspection shows the BOAT has broad arches sweeping across the face of the three-towers-into-one building.

You may be wondering why anyone building such a massive structure would stop 3 feet short of an even 1,000 feet. The tower was originally designed to reach 1,005 feet (maybe to account for settling into Seattle's muddy foundation). However, the Federal Aviation Administration (FAA) required the builders to lower the building by 8 feet, presumably to allow planes sufficient clearance as they approach SeaTac International Airport. Maybe it's just me, but in the realm of jumbo jetliners, it doesn't seem that 8 feet would make all that much difference.

The intrepid designers wouldn't be deterred with regard to the number of floors, though. Instead of reducing the number of floors, they simply shortened each one by 6 inches. This explains why, although not the tallest building west of the Mississippi River, the BOAT has more floors.

Five thousand employees work in the tower. Its Columbia Club women's restroom was once selected America's Best Bathroom, and according to Tripadvisor.com, the BOAT alone contains more lawyers than the entire nation of Japan. Whether that's a good thing or bad, I'll leave up to you.

The Bank of America Tower is located at 701 Fifth Avenue.

Need Some GORE-TEX Jammies?

REI

Recreational Equipment Incorporated, or REI, is known in America and around the world as one of the premier outdoor recreational equipment outfitters. However, as with most giants, you may be unaware of its humble start. The first time I went into the original REI store, it was in a 37,000-square-foot, five-level operation located on 11th Avenue

between East Pike and East Pine Streets. I marveled at all the camping, climbing, and hiking gear.

Fast-forward to the present: REI now operates some ninety stores in twenty-five states across America. Although its corporate offices are now in Kent, about 20 miles south of Seattle, its flagship store sits along Interstate 5 at the edge of downtown Seattle. The store's massive indoor climbing rock and outdoor mountain bike test trail are clearly visible magnets.

The place is as beautiful as it is huge—over 80,000 square feet of every type of state-of-the-art outdoor gear and products you could imagine. From mountain climbing and camping gear to kayaks, bikes, and much more, you're bound to find something of interest—even if you simply enjoy that Seattle GORE-TEX look.

Lloyd and Mary Anderson founded the company in 1938, but not in the usual way. Rather than a traditional corporation, REI was set up as, and still is, a membership cooperative. I count myself among the 2.5 million active members and 8 million total members since it began doing business, making REI the largest consumer cooperative in the country.

REI offers fun inside Seattle's flagship store and out. Inside, you can test your rock climbing skills on a 110-ton, 65-foot indoor climbing pinnacle—the largest in the world—complete with instructors to assist you. Outside, you can test mountain bikes on a rugged storeside course. REI also operates a travel service that organizes biking, hiking, and kayaking trips to places like the Alps, Costa Rica, and New Zealand.

REI's flagship store is located at 222 Yale Avenue North. For more information call (206) 223-1944 or visit www.rei.com/stores/seattle.

Trivia

Seattle was the first city in the United States to play a Beatles song on the radio.

Hammering Home a Point
Hammering Man

If you've wandered the streets of downtown Seattle in the vicinity of the Seattle Art Museum (SAM), you've no doubt noticed a very large man with a fierce work ethic on the corner. This would be *Hammering Man*—not the most glamorous name, but it is an apt description.

You won't find a more diligent worker in all Seattle.

93

Installed on September 12, 1992, the 48-foot-tall, 22,000-pound, primer-black sculpture swings his hammer four times per minute almost every day from 7:00 a.m. to 10:00 p.m. *Hammering Man* gets only one day off per year—Labor Day. Incidentally, on Labor Day 1993 a group of artists attached a ball and chain to *Hammering Man*'s leg. We are left to our own imaginations to surmise the artists'/suspects' message.

Hammering Man's initial arrival and installation attempt in Seattle was inauspicious to say the least. On September 28, 1991, the crane's rigging broke, causing *Hammering Man* to fall. Although he fell only a foot, the damage was sufficient to send the large laborer back to his birthplace at a Connecticut foundry for emergency surgery.

Jonathan Borofsky, a Boston-born artist and *Hammering Man*'s creator, says he wanted to honor workers in the Northwest, who are known for working with their hands, whether it be assembling airplanes, cutting down trees, or fishing. Borofsky has deployed *Hammering Men* throughout the world. Seattle's is the second largest; his larger cousin is located in Frankfurt, Germany.

Barofsky installed *Hammering Man* so that it appears he's standing directly on the ground without a base, in full contemplative view of pedestrians and drivers. Barofsky also hopes *Hammering Man* tickles the imaginations of children who see him and that it will cajole an interest within them to seek out other wonders that reside behind SAM's doors.

Hammering Man is located at First Avenue and University Street. For more information on the Seattle Art Museum, call (206) 625-8900 or visit www.seattleartmuseum.org.

Brrrrrrrr!

Puget Sound

Aside from the mountains, Puget Sound is the most defining natural feature of the Seattle area. Brit George Vancouver explored the sound in 1792, and while many seafaring captains of that era had reputations for inflated egos, Vancouver named the body of water for a second lieutenant, Peter Puget, who had probed the main channel during the expedition.

Blessed with deepwater harbors, cities like Seattle, Tacoma, and Everett flourished. The primary seaway into the sound slips through the Strait of Juan de Fuca. The sound wraps its arms around the Kitsap Peninsula and several islands as it stretches approximately 100 miles south to the Port of Olympia. More than half the population of Washington lives in the Puget Sound region.

So what's so curious about Puget Sound? Well, did you know that it offers world-class scuba diving? Diving instructor extraordinaire, Brian Wiederspan, taught Jody and me to dive in Puget Sound—oh, did I mention, in COLD, Puget Sound? Brrrrrrrr! However, wear a good, thick, wet or dry suit and you'll be fine. Winter is best; less algae means better visibility.

My wife had enjoyed our dives in the frigid Sound—until we dove in warm Maui waters. After diving in the Sound with what seemed like 2-inch-thick wetsuits, peering into 3- to 15-foot visibility, our Hawaii experience ruined Puget Sound for Jody. She'll still dive with me, just as long as it's preceded by a westbound flight on Hawaiian Airlines.

All kidding aside, Puget Sound offers a great adventure for divers, who can explore wrecks and see the biggest and most spectacularly colored starfish, octopuses, sea cucumbers, and, on occasion, a baby seal.

To reach a diving location, head west from anywhere in Seattle until you begin gulping salt water.

Holy Moly!
St. James Cathedral

A. M. A. Blanchet, the Catholic Diocese of Nesqually's (Seattle) first bishop, uttered a curiously frank comment to Father Francis Xavier Prefontaine, the priest determined to minister to the resistant Catholic pioneers of early Seattle. Anyone overhearing the bishop's biting remark would never have guessed that Seattle would someday be home to the magnificent, Italian Renaissance–inspired St. James Cathedral.

What exactly did Bishop Blanchet say to the eager Father Francis Xavier regarding Catholics in the fledgling city? "Seattle is a lost cause."

The focal points of the cathedral's architecture are two great towers and a massive dome, which face west toward Elliot Bay. The dome was described as "practically" indestructible; the caveat was proved on February 2, 1916, when the dome caved in under the weight of a heavier than normal snowfall. One story has it that the church hierarchy, concerned that folks in the Protestant quarter might capitalize on the catastrophe as God choosing sides, warned the editor of the diocesan newspaper to not print the story.

Today St. James Cathedral continues to stand sentinel on the crest of the west slope of First Hill looking over the heart of downtown Seattle. It is a feast for the eyes both inside and out, with myriad nooks and crannies to explore.

I have many memories of professional visits to St. James, but one stands out. A man calling himself the reincarnation of Pope John Paul XVI (he said he was from the future) insisted that since he outranked the bishop, he needed to move into His Excellency's residence.

Even more memorable was an event demonstrating that my daughter Heather is unalterably a city girl. She had attended midnight Mass on Christmas at St. James Cathedral. On Christmas morning, when we asked her about the service—about the music, the decorations, the colors and lights—her jubilant response was, "I got such a great parking space!" I think she still thinks of it as a divine event.

St. James Cathedral is located at 804 Ninth Avenue. For more information call (206) 382-4280 or visit www.stjames-cathedral.org.

A Naval Battle—in Seattle?
The Battle of Seattle

Having grown up in New England, where the first battles of the American Revolution were fought, it wasn't unusual for us to play baseball on fields where Continental soldiers had marched. In the East, Civil War battlefields dot the countryside, and the West has such well-known battlefields as Little Big Horn. However, does anyone strolling along the cobblestones in Seattle's Pioneer Square know about the U.S. military battle that took place here a century and a half ago?

If you're standing in Pioneer Square or on Pill Hill, you're standing on a battlefield where, on January 26, 1856, a U.S. Navy warship, U.S. Marines, settlers, and their Indian allies battled Indian forces in a one-day clash against 200 to 2,000 Indians from various outlying tribes.

The battle was a part of the greater Puget Sound, or Yakima, War, which lasted several years. The battle occurred after a visit from Washington Territorial Governor Isaac Stevens, who claimed that the rumors of attacks were almost certainly false. Apparently not convinced, Indian agent Doc Maynard evacuated almost 450 "friendly" Indians to the west side of Puget Sound, at his own expense.

Seattle's First Hill absorbed the first volley of the battle. U.S. forces learned that hostile Indian forces led by Klakum were located at Tom Pepper's house at the crest of then-forested First Hill. The U.S.S. *Decatur* unleashed its howitzer on the area. I'm thinking the round hit near present-day City Hall.

Although eyewitnesses reported a swarm of bullets flying for almost the entire day, the hostile forces' trigger discipline was apparently in short supply. The U.S. military and civilian forces suffered only three losses. On the Indian side, one report had ten Indian warriors falling; a later report had enemy forces admitting to twenty-eight dead and eighty wounded. However, no Indian casualties were recovered.

Following the battle, Klakum and twenty other Indians were captured and ordered held for trial by Governor Stevens. On May 15 they were tried and acquitted by military court-martial—their actions deemed acts of legitimate warfare and therefore not criminal. The men were released once peace was officially declared.

A City's Music Box
Benaroya Hall

Benaroya Hall is acclaimed for many reasons. One of the more curious is how this building, created to host musical performances, particularly

those of the Seattle Symphony, is built smack in the heart of the throbbing din of downtown Seattle—directly over a rail and bus tunnel. To eliminate sound intrusion from the outside and below, the hall was constructed as a smaller concrete box supported by rubber dampening pads built within a larger exterior box.

The Benaroya, which spreads over a full city block, boasts two performance halls—one rectangular, the other circular. Every aspect of the facility has its guests' enjoyment in mind. The construction materials, the lighting, the surrounding artwork, and of course the music all conspire to seduce one's senses.

The stage house and floor are constructed of cherry wood to enhance the visual as well as auditory enjoyment for performers as well as the audience. The materials used for the surfaces of the hall provide exquisite acoustics, diffusing sound throughout the hall for the best musical experience possible. In fact, the panels within the hall are subdivided into smaller panels of varying sizes so that each one resonates with its own distinctive frequency.

Seattle is one of only a handful of cities in America with a major symphony, opera, and ballet. Prior to the Benaroya, they all had to share a venue, which limited the symphony's schedule flexibility and number of performances. The Benaroya now hosts more than 775 events during its season, including the symphony.

The fund drive to build Benaroya Hall raised an astonishing $159 million in private funds, the largest amount ever raised for an arts project in Washington State. You can also enjoy the facility when there are no performances. There's an art gallery, restaurant, gift shops, and the awe-inspiring Garden of Remembrance, which honors the almost 8,000 Washington residents who sacrificed their lives in the service of their country.

Benaroya Hall is located at 200 University Street. For more information call (206) 215-4747 or (866) 833-4747 or visit www.seattle symphony.org/benaroya/.

Can You See the Light?

Seattle's Lighthouses

Finding even a large city such as Seattle by sea might require seafaring by Braille if it weren't for Seattle's lighthouses. With its oft-gray skies and frequently foggy harbors, you probably won't be surprised to learn that Seattle has two lighthouses within its city limits, one to the city's north and one to the south.

To the south, the Alki Point Lighthouse began its luminous career in 1887 as a humble lamp atop a single post planted in beach land owned by Hans Hanson and Knud Olson, who had purchased the 320-acre parcel for $450. The U.S. Lighthouse Service hired Hans and paid him $15 a month to care for the light.

The Alki Point Lighthouse hard at work.

★ ★

Hans's son, Edmund, inherited the land and assumed the role of official lightkeeper when his dad died. In 1911 the Lighthouse Service purchased a 1.5-acre wedge of the original parcel from Edmund for just shy of $10,000. A foghorn was added along with an octagonal light tower in 1913.

To the north, rising from the beach sand below the natural beauty of Magnolia Bluff and Discovery Park, today's explorers can find the West Point Lighthouse, which began guiding ships in 1881. When the Washington Ship Canal was completed in 1917, the lighthouse also served as an entrance marker to the Ballard Locks, which lead vessels into Lakes Union and Washington.

The West Point Lighthouse was the last in the state to be automated, after having been manned for over a century. In 2004 Seattle acquired the property, and the city plans to restore the lighthouse and open it up to visitors. The facility is now part of Discovery Park, Seattle's largest city park.

Alki Point Lighthouse is located at Alki and 63rd Avenues. West Point Lighthouse is located at 3801 West Government Way in Discovery Park.

A Neighborhood Army Base

Fort Lawton

Can you imagine the city of Seattle and some private citizens donating more than 700 acres of land to the United States to build a military installation? Well, it happened in 1897 when land in the Magnolia neighborhood was donated to build Fort Lawton to defend Seattle against naval attack.

The land was chosen for its strategic view of Puget Sound's entrance to Elliot Bay. In 1900 the fort was officially named for Civil War and Spanish-American War veteran Major General Henry W. Lawton, who had recently died in the Philippines. The military established the fort for three primary reasons: Enemy vessels could easily harbor in Puget Sound; the ever-growing ports of Tacoma, Seattle, and Everett were easy targets; and there was a plan to build a ship canal from Puget Sound to Lake Washington that would be large enough for warships.

Fort Lawton has an eclectic history, to say the least. In 1938, due to larger facilities in Bremerton and at (then) Camp Lewis shouldering the weight of regional defense, the government offered the land back to the City of Seattle for a dollar. The city council declined the offer, fearing they couldn't bear the maintenance costs—a shrewd decision indeed.

World War II put value back into the property for government purposes. During the war, the fort was a San Francisco port of embarkation for as many as 20,000 troops shipping overseas. During and after the war, more than one million troops passed through Fort Lawton's gates. The fort was also a prisoner-of-war camp incarcerating more than 1,000 German prisoners of war (some of whom are buried here). It was also a holding facility for Italian prisoners on their way to military prison in Hawaii.

After WWII the base was used as an Air Force radar site and missile base before the military decided to surplus most of the base. In 1968, thanks to the efforts of U.S. Senator Henry M. (Scoop) Jackson, the military offered about 530 acres to the city to use for what would become Discovery Park.

A small portion of land survives as Fort Lawton. The best-preserved group of buildings were designated a landmark district in 1988, and the base is currently home to the 70th Regional Readiness Command—a 3,000-soldier unit known as the Trailblazers.

Fort Lawton is located in Discovery Park, 3801 West Government Way.

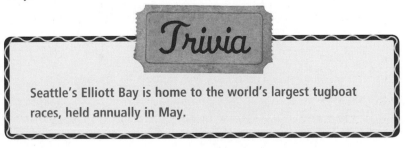

Trivia

Seattle's Elliott Bay is home to the world's largest tugboat races, held annually in May.

★ ★

The Spaciest Needle-iest of Them All

Space Needle

Everything that can be written about the Space Needle has been written, right? Hold on. I thought so, too, until I remembered what a writing guru once wrote: "It's not yours until you write about it." So it's my turn to write about the Emerald City's most identifiable and beloved landmark—one of the most recognizable structures in the world.

The Space Needle, Seattle's de facto logo, is one of the most recognizable structures on Earth.

Here are a few things you may not have known: The Space Needle was built in less than a year because backers were almost unable to secure a plot of land upon which to erect it before the World's Fair;

three people have committed suicide by leaping off the observation deck; and the foundation is a 30-foot-deep, 6,000-ton block of concrete and steel. This base weighs approximately the same as the structure aboveground, placing its center of balance at lower than the height of the average adult human being.

Seventy-two massive, 30-foot-long bolts anchor the spire to its base. The Needle has twenty-five lightening rods at the top, including the tower. Since 1982 the Space Needle has become the West Coast's premier New Year's Eve celebration spot, with a spectacular fireworks show exploding off the top. And on New Year's Eve 1999, a brand-new Skybeam was illuminated, its beacon blasting 85 million candle power into the night sky.

Appropriately, the elevators descend at the speed of a raindrop, 10 miles per hour. But perhaps even more interesting, if not quite as apt for a city that rarely sees snow (which falls at 3 miles per hour), if you ride the elevator during a snowfall, the flakes will appear to fall upward.

Get this: A stork's nest was originally planned for the top of the Space Needle. Seattleites, passionate as ever about the environment, haven't always thought things through. They ran into one tiny, albeit insurmountable obstacle: Storks don't, and can't, live in Seattle's climate.

And what's the most infamous event in Space Needle history? On April Fool's Day 1989, a local comedy show, KING TV's *Almost Live,* aired a "Special Report" that the Space Needle had fallen over. Emergency lines were jammed, a la *War of the Worlds,* and the Space Needle received more than 700 phone calls. Folks could have been forgiven except for the flashing alert on the screen notifying viewers that the report was a prank.

The Space Needle is located at 400 Broad Street, right in the heart of Seattle Center. For more information call (206) 905-2100 or visit www.spaceneedle.com.

★ ★

To the Needle and Back a Gazillion Times
Seattle Center Monorail

Having ridden the monorail many times and having just ridden it a couple of days ago during our annual Christmas family outing, I can attest to the continuing popularity of the historic single-rail train—standing room only.

The Seattle Center Monorail takes you from Westlake Mall to the Space Needle in the blink of an eye.

Okay, for the particulars: The Seattle Center monorail is the first and, at 50 miles per hour, fastest full-size monorail in America. It's also the only fully self-sufficient public transit line in the nation. This recently designated Seattle historic landmark opened for the 1962 World's Fair on March 24 of that year, and eight million passengers rode the train during the fair's six-month run. Today about two and a half million passengers ride annually. A monorail trip from Seattle Center to or from Westlake Mall takes two minutes and leaves every ten minutes. When two trains operate for special events, a train leaves every five minutes. The train, which the Experience Music Project appears to be swallowing as it arrives at the Seattle Center Grounds, can carry 450 passengers.

Although the monorail has been plagued in recent years by relatively minor collisions and a fire in which no serious injuries were reported, the monorail-related curiosity I'm most familiar with is one in which I participated. During a special event in Seattle back in the mid-1990s, my partner and I, along with another two-officer team, were assigned to ride the monorail for several hours. Back and forth and back and forth; I never thought I would tire of the ride, but . . .

I think it was somewhere around trip number twenty-two or twenty-five when my partner, who, by the way, is an accomplished schmoozer, nearly convinced the monorail operator to allow him to drive one trip. She eventually relented, promising, "If we have an empty trip (no passengers except for us four officers), I'll let you drive."

We were nearing the end of our assignment, and each trip had fewer passengers. On one of the last trips, it appeared we'd finally have an empty train. The operator was just about to close the doors when one gentleman skittered through the ticket booth and onto the train. So close.

The Seattle Center Monorail runs between Seattle Center and Westlake Mall. For more information, including schedules, call (206) 905-2620 or visit www.seattlemonorail.com.

You Always Remember Your First
Denny Park

I'm not certain if Denny Park, Seattle's first municipal park, had an auspicious or an inauspicious beginning. Why? It was Seattle's first municipal cemetery before it became its first park.

In the 1860s David Denny granted the city use of the property for a cemetery. In July 1883 Denny donated the six-acre parcel to the city for use as a public park. But what about those poor deceased Seattle pioneers? Workers transported most of the remains to the Washelli Cemetery on Capitol Hill. Those poor folks were moved once again when that cemetery, in turn, became Volunteer Park.

During what's known as the Denny Regrade, workers flattened the park, which had originally been 60 feet higher. Following this razing, the grounds were replanted with gardens and trees.

The Seattle Department of Parks and Recreation built its head-quarters along the park's west side. Although the Denny family had opposed the construction of the building, the American Institute of Architects awarded the facility top honors for its design. The parks department still uses the building today.

Denny Park is located at 100 Dexter Avenue North. For more information call (206) 684-4075 or visit www.cityofseattle.net/parks/parkdetail.asp?ID=309.

High School Football and So Much More
Memorial Stadium

Memorial Stadium is a sports venue dedicated to Seattle high school students killed in World War II. A shrine dedicated to these students stands sentinel at the east entrance, and engraved upon the memorial's face are the names of the students—a reminder that freedom isn't free.

I'm not sure there's another high school stadium in America that has a more varied history. It hosted the opening ceremonies of the 1962 World's Fair. Five thousand seats were added to the 12,000-seat stadium in 1975, when the Seattle Sounders of the North American Soccer League called it their home field. Many years later, a reconstituted Sounders team played here before moving to their new, shared digs at Qwest Field. Concerts are still held here occasionally, especially during large festivals, such as Bumbershoot.

In addition to its professional past, the stadium remains the home field for high school football teams within the Seattle School District. In fact, although the stadium sits within the Seattle Center grounds, the facility is owned and maintained by the school district.

On a personal note (you knew I had one), the largest annual charity football game in America used to be held in Seattle each fall, pitting the Seattle Police Department Badgers against the Tacoma P. D. Hogs. Never having played football—my high school had only a soccer team—when my oldest son was playing high school football, I saw the charity event as an opportunity for bonding.

During the year I "played" on the team, practices were held at Memorial Stadium. Although I wasn't the best athlete in the world, after practicing exclusively with the offense as an eighth-stringer or so, the defensive coach snuck me into the official game for three plays at the end of our loss. And so my illustrious football career came to an end.

Memorial Stadium is located at Fifth Avenue and Harrison Street, northeast Seattle Center. For more information call (206) 252-1800.

No Adults Allowed without a Responsible Child

The Seattle Children's Museum

In 1979 some cool parents had the idea that kids might enjoy a museum of their own where they weren't constantly being told, "Don't touch that," "Keep your hands in your pockets," and "Don't make me come over there." So the Seattle Children's Museum (SCM) was born.

In 1981 the SCM's first exhibit found a home within the Wing Luke Museum, a popular destination in Seattle's Chinatown. The exhibit, called "A Children's Place," focused on Chinese culture. Later that year the SCM opened its first facility in Pioneer Square.

In 1985 SCM moved to its present location in the shadow of the Space Needle on the first floor of the Center House, smack in the middle of the Seattle Center grounds. Interestingly, the museum

occupies the ground terminus of the Bubbleator—Seattle's famous 1962 World's Fair clear-dome elevator.

The SCM allows children from the crib to ten years old to learn, not only by seeing and hearing but also by doing. The museum complements its permanent exhibits with traveling exhibits. The permanent exhibits include the Bijou Theatre, Cog City, Discovery Bay, Global Village, Imagination Studio, Go Figure, Mountain Forest, and Neighborhood.

And you adults best remember: If you have a notion to go to the museum solo, forget about it—you won't be allowed in unless accompanied by a responsible child.

The Seattle Children's Museum is located at 305 Harrison Street. For more information call (206) 441-1768 or visit www.thechildrens museum.org/.

A Splashing Treat for Eyes and Ears
International Fountain

Like so many other features at Seattle Center, the "Singing Fountain," as many Seattleites like to call it, was originally created for the 1962 World's Fair. The fountain sits surrounded by a lush grassy carpet in the shadow of the Space Needle between Key Arena and the Center House. This unique fountain not only does what we'd expect—spray streams of water—but also plays music, which bursts forth from a chamber within.

The fountain's original fire hose nozzle–looking fixtures protruding from its half-dome shape made it resemble a robotic sea urchin floating in a sea of white rock. Kids back then invented a game where they'd run over the rocks and onto the fountain and attempt to place a cup onto the nozzle before the water shot into their faces.

In 1995 the fountain was completely redone, but I was impressed that the builders maintained the spirit of the old fountain. Instead of rocks, there's now smooth pavement; and the half-dome fountain, its

Of Course Seattle Is the Rainiest City in America— Right?

Seattle is America's rainiest city, right? Well . . . in a 2007 MSNBC list of the most saturated cities in the contiguous forty-eight states, the Emerald City doesn't even crack the top twenty-five. Seattle is less than impressive as America's forty-fourth rainiest city. Well, Chicago isn't America's windiest city, either—so there.

The presumption that Seattle is the Rain King, over cities that get buckets more precipitation, is due to the manner in which the rain falls. Technically, Mobile, Alabama, may get more rain—but let me tell you, as the late Paul Harvey used to say, "the rest of the story." While Mobile averages 67 inches of rain annually over fifty-seven days, Seattle's seemingly puny 37 inches a year fall over a whopping 158 days. Add to that at least 226 days per year with at least some cloud cover, and I believe the mystery is solved.

surface now smooth, looks as though it has gotten a crew cut. The place-the-cup-on-the-nozzle game can no longer be enjoyed. However, it's now safer for kids to run around and onto the fountain, still emitting sharp shrieks as the streams of water spew out to strains of what Seattle Center staff refer to as world music.

The International Fountain is located at 305 Harrison Street. For more information call (206) 684-7200.

★ ★

The International, or "Singing," Fountain serenades you with music from around the world as you dodge the shooting streams of water.

Not *Bumper*shoot, *Bumber*shoot!

Bumbershoot Festival

Bumbershoot, BumberSHOOT, BUMBERSHOOT—not Bumpershoot! I hope this is the final word on this issue, which, if you couldn't tell, is one of my longest-standing pet peeves. For folks who wonder, bumbershoot has a specific meaning, which is fitting for a Seattle event. *Bumbershoot* is another word for *umbrella*. Its precise origin is murky, but regardless of its lexiconic pedigree, just pronounce it correctly—okay?

Bumbershoot began in 1971 and was originally known as the Mayor's Arts Festival, which was held in August. Today Bumbershoot is one of the largest cultural arts and music festivals in America and is held each Labor Day weekend at the Seattle Center grounds.

Some of the biggest names in music have appeared here over the decades, including Emmylou Harris, Chuck Berry, Ray Charles, Etta James, the Eurythmics, James Brown, Tina Turner, B. B. King, the

Ramones, Kanye West, REM, Fats Domino, Bonnie Raitt, Miles Davis, Roy Orbison, and Robert Cray.

One of the more interesting tidbits associated with Bumbershoot was from a 1999 essay by Paul Dorpat entitled, simply, *Bumbershoot.* Dorpat tells the story of Bumbershoot Festival literary arts coordinator Carol Orlock, who in 1977 phoned renowned science fiction author Isaac Asimov at his home on the East Coast and asked if he'd be interested in coming to Seattle to read excerpts from his stories. Upon realizing that Seattle is a fair distance from New York and would require flying, the master of stories that often included interstellar travel politely declined—he absolutely refused to fly.

Bumbershoot is held over Labor Day weekend on the Seattle Center grounds. For more information call (206) 281-7788 or visit www .bumbershoot.org.

Paul's Salute to Jimi
Experience Music Project

You can't talk about the inside of the Experience Music Project (EMP) without first talking about the outside, which defies you to ignore it. I often thought, *What the heck?,* during its construction. As the brightly colored "skin" was stretched over the skeleton, I once told my wife, "It looks like a kid melted some toys on the stove."

To say I wasn't immediately enamored with the design would be an understatement. I looked askance at the arcane, or esoteric, building. Was it created unusually for pure art's sake or to kidnap folks' attention? Of course some would argue that one facet of art is simply to be different, perhaps to offend, to shock, to grab people by their lapels and scream, "LOOK AT ME!" In that case, good job!

When I heard that people, including the building's architect, Frank O. Gehry, said the building was inspired by a smashed Stratocaster guitar, I reconsidered my disenchantment. Somehow this design now made sense—well, in a Pete Townsend–Kurt Cobain sort of way.

Since EMP opened in 2000, hordes of music-minded visitors have made their way here. At this museum you don't stand behind a velvet

★ ★

Don't forget to get your photo taken with this
life-size statue of the incomparable Jimi. Come on,
don't be shy—everyone else is doing it.

rope to admire from afar. This is the petting zoo of music museums,
with interpretive and interactive exhibitions that push the technological
envelope and take visitors out of the role of simple viewers and make
them participants—musicians for a moment.

Please allow enough time to fully absorb what the 40,000-square-
foot museum has to offer. The idea began with Paul Allen's notion to
share his collection of Jimi Hendrix memorabilia, so it's appropriate that
the hippie-styled "Sky Church" dominates the interior with the biggest
flat-screen TV you've ever seen. You'll also find homage paid to many
other rock icons, a restaurant, the Sci-Fi Hall of Fame, and a bookstore.

The final steel beam installed bears the signatures of the construction workers on site that day. If you want a legal way to "sneak" into
EMP, ride the monorail as it cruises right through the museum on its
trek to and from the Seattle Center.

Some observers think the multicolored EMP building looks like a melted toy.

Experience Music Project is located at 325 Fifth Avenue North. For more information call (206) 770-2700 or visit www.empsfm.org.

Hippie Heaven
Northwest Folklife Festival

The Northwest Folklife Festival, America's largest free community arts festival, is the most visible offspring of the nonprofit organization known as Northwest Folklife, founded in 1972 to promote the traditional, cultural, and ethnic heritage of Pacific Northwest communities.

The festival, which welcomes a quarter million visitors annually, is held over Memorial Day weekend as a beginning-of-summer bookend to its end-of-summer counterpart, Bumbershoot, which is held on Labor Day weekend. Both events are held on the Seattle Center grounds.

This festival includes so many participants of such varied arts that it's hard to adequately relate the flavor of the event. Then I went to the

festival's Web site, and while I found the "vitals" of the event interesting, I found the brief descriptions of participating artists' music posi-
tively fascinating.

Even without naming the specific artists, or even specific musical
styles, you'll get a sense of the breadth and depth of this event from
the following blurbs:

- Banjo Andy/The Crusty Minstrel (I suppose it could have been,
  Crusty Andy/The Banjo Minstrel)
- Exciting and Dazzling Feet! (Both exciting and dazzling feet? I'm
  highly suspicious.)
- 150 Feet of Fury and Grace (Is that 75 dancers, or 150 feet of
  dancers measured side by side?)
- The Microbrew of Music (Not at all sure what to make of this one.)
- Russian Bellydance Master (How 'bout just Russian Belly Master?)
- Late-Blooming Polyglot Busker (Or Procrastinating Multilingual
  Wastrel. See—two can play at this game.)
- Armor-Piercing Balkan Brass (Best not to resist this music!)
- Frontporch Music w/a Backbeat (Wonder what you'd find on the
  back porch?)
- Egyptian Cabaret Bellydancing (I literally can't describe what I'm
  seeing in my head.)
- 1960s Style Hootenanny (Perfectly descriptive; come prepared to
  sing along.)

The Northwest Folklife Festival is held over Memorial Day weekend
on the Seattle Center grounds. For more information call (206) 684-
7300 or visit www.nwfolklife.org/.

Don't Forget to Duck
Ride the Duck

Now this is not a uniquely Seattle curiosity, but check out the name—
it should be, shouldn't it? In fact, anything with "duck" in the
title—ever—should be associated with Seattle. Longtime Seattleites

will remember a skit on the *Almost Live* local TV comedy-sketch show, which often highlighted Seattle's cultural quirks. The skit, "Ballard Vice," was a send-up of the show *Miami Vice,* featuring Seattle's Ballard community in Miami's place. The skit replaced *Miami Vice*'s opening credits scene, showing a flock of elegant pink flamingoes flowing along the beach, with a bunch of goofy ducks waddling toward a lake—now that's vintage Seattle.

So, there you have Seattle's duck bona fides, and now back to duck talk. Although other cities have similar amphibious vehicle rides, which operate both on land and in the water, Seattle's Ride the Duck company boasts a small fleet of actual vintage WWII landing craft known as DUKWs (D–1942, U–amphibious 2.5 ton, K–front-wheel drive, W–rear-wheel drive).

The craft originally accommodated twenty-five battle-clad soldiers. Today it comfortably accommodates thirty-six variously clad tourists, who may only have to worry about ducking droppings from an occasional errant seagull.

If you want to see the city in a truly Seattle way, then riding the duck definitely fits the bill. And remember Ride the Duck's motto: "She's not very fast, but she's better in the water than any truck, and she'll beat any boat on the highway!"

Ride the Duck is located at 516 Broad Street. For more information call (206) 441-DUCK (3825) or (800) 817-1116 or visit www.ridethe ducksofseattle.com.

Where Learning Is Just Plain Fun
Pacific Science Center

If you belong to that subspecies of Homo sapiens who thinks museums are so dull that you seriously can't decide between spending a day staring at what some pretentious dolt tells you is interesting and sticking your face in a bucket of broken glass, have I got a museum for you.

The Pacific Science Center began as the United States Science Pavilion for the 1962 World's Fair. Designed by Minoru Yamasaki, who

★ ★

The Pacific Science Center—a lot more fun
than your average museum!

also designed New York's World Trade Center, the science center has
evolved into the authority on how to enthrall people of all ages with
their approachable vision of science. "Don't touch it, you'll break it"
doesn't apply here.

Try just a small sampling of what this wonderful curiosity has to
offer. Do you like IMAX films? The Pacific Science Center is one of the
few places on Earth with two IMAX theaters, with one being one of
the largest dome theaters in the world. And let's take a look at the
calendar, which alone leaves one stunned and hard-pressed to choose
what to see first. A sampling for the present month includes Sultry Science: a night of cocktails and aphrodisiac-inspired hors d'oeuvres. At a
museum? At this museum, yep! You could even get a lip-print reading
by a professional lipsologist.

There's Model Railroad Weekend, an exclusive one-week premier
U23D IMAX concert featuring the Irish rock band U2, a Valentine's Day

slumber party, a seminar on planning your own snowshoeing expedition, and a bunch more. Like what? How about taking a "Journey through Time" with dinosaurs of the Mesozoic era? Or you can breeze through the Tropical Butterfly House, creep through the insect village, wade into a model of Puget Sound and saltwater tidepool, get on TV as a guest meteorologist at the Kids Works exhibit, and visit a colony of East African naked mole rats.

The Pacific Science Center is located at 200 Second Avenue North. For more information call (206) 443-2001 or visit www.pacsci.org.

Check Out These Twinkle Toes
Pacific Northwest Ballet

Whenever possible, I've personally experienced the people, places, and things I describe for you in this book. However, I must now defer to my wife, Jody, as I've never attended the ballet. I'm not really a ballet kind of guy, although I truly appreciate the talent and effort and enjoy much of the music.

Jody and our daughter Heather have made a Christmas tradition of Kent Stowell's and Maurice Sendak's collaboratively brilliant presentation of *The Nutcracker,* enjoying the performance every year since 1992. Jody purchases a new "nutcracker" for Heather at each show. Heather now commands her own little brigade of nutcrackers, which guard her Christmas tree each December. Over the years, more than 1.5 million people have joined them at these performances.

The company was founded in 1972 as the Pacific Northwest Dance Association and changed its name to the Pacific Northwest Ballet in 1978. The progress over the years has been spectacular for what has become one of the five-largest and one of the most acclaimed ballet companies in America. The ballet—which has grown from 1,200 subscribers in 1977, with a budget of $800,000, to more than 10,000 subscribers—is said to have the highest per-capita attendance of any major ballet in the United States and has an annual budget of $19 million.

Their repertoire includes nearly one hundred classic and new ballets. The ballet initially toured regionally, but today the ballet also performs nationally and internationally. Its international performances have delighted audiences around the globe, and in 2006 the ballet was chosen to perform at the prestigious Fall for Dance festival at New York City's New York Center.

Aside from operating its own school for serious dance students from kindergarten through high school, the company offers a Dancer Transition Program in conjunction with Seattle University designed to assist its dancers with "life after dance" (although some dancers might argue that there is no life after dance).

The company maintains three state-of-the-art facilities: magnificent McCaw Hall; the Phelps Center at Seattle Center; and the Francis Russell Center, a 24,000-square-foot facility housing four dance studios and two conditioning studios.

Pacific Northwest Ballet is located at 301 Mercer Street. For more information call (206) 441-9411 or visit www.pnb.org.

How Did It Ever Get Its Name?

Mural Amphitheater

The Mural Amphitheater, built for the 1962 World's Fair, is composed of a mural, which is a mosaic created by artist Paul Horiuchi; a stage that was once a reflecting pool; and a grassy knoll that used to be—well, a grassy knoll.

The facility, considered a midsize venue, is used during the Folklife Festival and Bumbershoot for music and comedy performances. The stage, backed by the mural, lies in the shadow of the Space Needle—if the sun is actually shining.

As you walk by during a performance, the music calls to you. You stroll over, find yourself a patch of green, and simply sit down to enjoy a show. I remember delaying going to a show at the IMAX theater once, waylaid by the sounds of the band Junior Cadillac.

Over the years many performers have cast shadows onto the mural

The Mural Amphitheater, a performance venue since the 1962 World's Fair, sits beneath the Space Needle.

from the venerable stage, including a few local bands. Perhaps you've heard of them: Nirvana, Pearl Jam, and Alice in Chains.

In August 2007 this city of Seattle landmark was also used for Movies at the Mural, when free movies were played for a first-come, first-served audience. Another nice feature about this venue is that it's close to the Center House—and the restrooms and vendors inside.

The World's Not Always Fair, but This Was
1962 World's Fair

If the Klondike gold rush in 1889 and the Alaska-Yukon-Pacific Exposition in 1909 put Seattle on the national map, it was the 1962 World's

★ ★

Fair—Century 21 that put it on the world map. The fair's legacy continues today with the immensely popular Space Needle and Seattle Center Monorail. Over three and a half million people, including one Al Rochester, attended the exposition, held on the University of Washington campus.

By 1955 Rochester had become a city councilman and was in a position to propose that a world's fair be held in Seattle. With momentum on his side, the site we all know today was chosen from among many larger sites. A bond was approved in a lopsided affirmative vote, and the "Festival of the West" was born. That dorky name was soon changed to Century 21.

Influenced by the Soviets' recent successes in space, planners decided the theme of the fair would be the future and modern science education. The emphasis would be on "approachable" science that both science geeks and average Joes, and Josephines, could appreciate.

State and federal politicians, scientists, and politician-scientists such as future governor Dixy Lee Ray (a marine biologist) got involved. In fact, the U.S. government kicked in ten million bucks to build a proper science pavilion, which we know today as the beloved Pacific Science Center.

The last thing needed to make it a true World's Fair was the blessing of the Bureau of International Exhibitions in Paris, France. New York City was also competing for this recognition, but the Seattle representative's Northwest charms outshone the New York contingent's arrogance. Seattle received the certification securing a true World's Fair for the city.

A Lighthou . . . ship?

The Lightship *Swiftsure*

You may have already figured out that a lightship is essentially a floating lighthouse. It serves the same purpose as a land-based lighthouse but has the additional advantage of being mobile, for use where most needed at any given time. The *Swiftsure* LV83 served our nation in

For your traveling coastal needs—here's a lighthouse when and where you need one.

more capacities than originally intended from her birth in 1904 to her decommissioning in 1960. She apparently got her name from a temporary assignment at Swiftsure Bank near Cape Flattery on the Columbia River at the Washington-Oregon border.

The *Swiftsure* was launched in Camden, New Jersey, before it sailed around the tip of South America, headed for service on America's West Coast. Among her first assignments, the lightship guided sea traffic through the persistently dense fog into San Francisco Bay. Understandably, it was during this service that a foghorn was added.

During World War II, the U.S. Navy appropriated the ship from the Coast Guard for wartime service. Guns were mounted at several locations on the ship, which was repainted battleship gray. Its quarters were expanded to accommodate a crew of forty sailors.

The ship finished its long career serving along the Washington coast. The *Swiftsure* is one of the three oldest surviving lightships in the United States and the only one still fitted with its original steam engines. The ship was awarded National Landmark status and can be visited at the old wooden boat center at the south end of Lake Union.

The *Swiftsure* is berthed at the Center for Wooden Boats, 1010 Valley Street.

Location, Location, Location

Pyramid Alehouse

One of the best reasons—outside of their fantastic brews—to visit Pyramid Alehouse, Brewery, and Restaurant is its location. It sits conveniently close to the waterfront and Pioneer Square. But more important, it's directly across the street from Safeco Field, home of the Seattle Mariners, and kitty-corner to Qwest Field, home of the Seattle Seahawks and Seattle Sounders.

You'd be hard-pressed to find better hosts for an outing in downtown Seattle, especially at game time. A few weeks ago we had out-of-town family visiting. We took in a baseball game, but first we needed a good location to meet and to get a bite; of course we chose Pyramid. It was packed, but we were seated in a cozy nook on the second floor. I had my digits curled around an ice-cold Hefeweizen in no time.

Even if we had to wait, we could have done it in Pyramid's "Left Out Field" beer garden, located in front of the building. With apologies to Mariners' fans, we were actually going to the game to watch the Red Sox. As it turned out, we wound up watching the Sox lose. Seems that regardless of standings, the Mariners seem to have the Sox's number. Perhaps the Red Sox players are spending too much time at Pyramid's beer garden before the game.

Pyramid was one of the first microbreweries in the country. It began brewing in 1984 as a part of Hart Brewing, producing Pyramid Ales.

In 1989 a group of beer devotees from Seattle bought the company, changing the corporate name in 1996 to Pyramid Breweries.

Pyramid Alehouse, Brewery, and Restaurant is located at 1201 First Avenue South. For more information call (206) 682-3377 or visit www .pyramidbrew.com.

Seattle's Biggest Bumbershoot
Safeco Field's Ball Cap

The birth of Safeco Field, "The Safe," was controversial, but one element of the baseball park that is uncontroversial is its stunning beauty. Safeco Field was built to emulate the great ballparks of the past, and as someone who grew up in New England watching ball games at Fenway Park, I can tell you there's nothing like watching a game in a traditional ballpark. (Although, sometimes I miss washing down a mustard-slathered King Dog with an ice-cold King Beer at the cavernous King Dome.)

Safeco Field's roof opens and closes— kind of like a giant umbrella.

Seattle's Gentleman of Sports

If you've ever wondered, while traveling between Safeco Field and Qwest Field, why the city would name the street for an American luxury car, you're not alone. Or perhaps you thought South Royal Brougham Way had simply been tagged with a snooty British-sounding appellation. And even if these weren't your thoughts, unless you're a very longtime Seattleite, did you know that Royal Brougham was a person—in fact, an exceptionally distinguished person?

Actually, it's apropos that the street passing between Seattle's two world-class sports venues be named for Brougham. The venerable journalist spent almost seventy years involved in one way or another with Seattle sports, with sixty-two years at the *Seattle Post-Intelligencer* newspaper.

From all accounts, Brougham was the consummate sports fan, philanthropist, and gentleman, who brought to Seattle such sports legends as Babe Ruth, Jack Dempsey, and Jesse Owens for charitable causes.

As reported in the *Post-Intelligencer:* "The 84-year-old collapsed in the King Dome press box, and as he was being rushed to a waiting aid car, Brougham tugged on the elevator operator's pant leg, moment's from death, and asked a question that describes this wonderful man so eloquently, 'What's the score?'"

Safeco Field holds a special significance for me. Prior to opening day, the field had a dress rehearsal. The Seattle Arsenal and Chaffee baseball teams, comprising seventeen- and eighteen-year-old boys, played an "official" game in Safeco Field. My son Bryan played for the Seattle team. This provided ballpark staff with an opportunity to work out any "bugs" before opening day—not to mention giving the kids the thrill of their early baseball careers.

As the kids came up to bat, each baseball player was introduced as a pro player as the rosters of the Seattle Mariners and San Diego Padres were displayed on the giant video screen. Of course the luckiest kid of the day was the player introduced as Ken Griffey Jr.!

Although no one tagged one out of the park that game, the kids played some good baseball and had the time of their lives. The game worked out well for the Safeco Field staff as well. One crucial element of the dress rehearsal was testing the massive retractable roof during game conditions. The three-paneled "umbrella" covers 8.75 acres, is 215 feet high, and weighs an incredible 22 million pounds. It takes the amazing structure twenty minutes to roll open or closed along enormous rails.

We learned that if the weather changes from rain to sunshine, it's best to leave the roof closed. That's because as the roof opens in sunshine, it drags a shadow across the field. This plays havoc with the players as they fight to handle baseballs that "disappear" into the shade or suddenly "reappear" into bright sunlight.

Safeco Field is located at 1250 First Avenue South, next to Quest Field in the south end of downtown Seattle. For more information on Safeco Field and the Seattle Mariners, visit http://seattle.mariners.mlb.com/sea/ballpark/index.jsp.

The Taj Mahal It Wasn't

Kingdome

I remember several distinct Seattle-isms friends told me about when I first arrived in the city. Like how the (then) Seafirst Tower was known locally as "the box the Space Needle came in"; how to use "Jesus Christ Made Seattle Under Protest" to remember Seattle's primary downtown streets; and that the Kingdome was Seattle's wart.

★ ★

Seattle always had a love-hate relationship with its concrete blemish, which was finally imploded in 2000 after twenty-four years of service. In general it was a terribly uncomfortable place to watch a sporting event, especially baseball. This condition was somewhat mitigated for football by the fact that the Dome, being the largest freestanding concrete structure in the world, was freakin' loud.

The Dome was perennially known as the loudest stadium in the NFL. Even though we poor Seahawks fans didn't always have a whole lot to hoot and holler about back then, we are great football fans and we loved our Kingdome-era Seahawks. Jim Zorn, Steve Largent, Kenny Easley, and Coach Knox, to name a few, are remembered fondly.

Here are a few Kingdome curiosities for ya: Although the Kingdome cost $67 million to build in 1976, $70 million was spent in 1994 just to fix the roof. The stadium hosted the 1979 MLB All-Star Game; Gaylord Perry won the 300th game of his career in 1982 here; Randy Johnson and Chris Bosio pitched no-hitters on this field; and baseball history was made here when Ken Griffey Sr. and Ken Griffey Jr. started a game in the same outfield, making them the first father and son to take the field together as players in a major league baseball game.

A few other interesting tidbits: What goes up must come down. Right? Well, not so much. Two foul balls went up but never came back down; both got stuck in a speaker, and both were ruled strikes. While the Kingdome's short field would normally have been considered a hitter's ballpark, hitters were thwarted by its air-conditioning system. The air-conditioning units and vents actually blew air toward the infield, taking a bit of the mojo off some fly balls that might otherwise have been dingers. And here's the last, least, and just plain curious: When the Mariners first began playing in the Kingdome, the outfield distances were marked on the fences in both feet and fathoms.

The Bean That Launched a Craze
Starbucks

The master of the java universe certainly doesn't need free advertising, but to not include Starbucks in a book about Seattle would be

A Striking Distinction

Two days before Christmas 1975, Seattle Police Officer Ray Johnson was standing in a checkout line at a market when a robbery suspect entered the store and displayed a gun. Officer Johnson lunged for the gun, fought with the suspect, but was unable to keep him from firing the weapon.

The suspect emptied his .38 caliber pistol, striking Johnson in his hand and getting off two rounds to Johnson's chest before fleeing. Johnson suffered a severe wound to his hand but suffered only bruising to his chest. Johnson became the first law enforcement officer in America to be saved by wearing soft body armor made of a material called Kevlar.

That year Kevlar body armor saved the lives of seventeen other officers nationwide, and today the vast majority of law enforcement officers across America don body armor before beginning their patrol shifts.

My guess is that Officer Johnson had the highest praise for the body armor that day. And I'm certain neither he nor his family found a better Christmas gift under the tree than that Kevlar vest!

like inserting a blank page in the middle—the omission would be as conspicuous as a Starbucks sign missing the siren peeking out of the center.

Siren? No, not the kind attached to the top of my patrol car. I'm talking about the half fish–half woman peeking out from the center of the Starbucks logo. You know the one that caused that fracas with its highly provocative "stick-figure" nakedness that compromised the sensibilities of some apparently peculiarly sensitive folks.

I'm not sure you'll find many cops who don't have a fondness for the Seattle original. Of course I don't think you'd find many cops without a fond disposition for coffee in general—along with a good ol' doughnut—but that might just be a stereotype. Well, let me amend that a bit, since we are talking about Seattle. In Seattle I believe it's a latté and a croissant.

The first Starbucks opened in 1971 in the Pike Place Market, the first of well over 10,000 now percolating around the world today. The original—not in its precise original location but only about a block away—still operates at 1912 Pike Place, where you can still sip your piping hot, or refreshingly cold, elixir de bean today. Don't be fooled, though; if you're looking for the ubiquitous green Starbucks sign, you won't find it. The sign outside the original store is brown.

The "original" Starbucks is located at 1912 Pike Place. For more information call (206) 448-8762 or visit www.starbucks.com.

So You Want Some Chinese, Do Ya?
Wing Luke Asian Museum

I first toured the Wing Luke Asian Museum when my children were in grade school. Although I hadn't felt that way at the time, it was my good fortune to have been tagged as a chaperone for my son's school field trip to Chinatown.

Having been a huge Bruce Lee fan and an admirer of Asian culture, the excursion was a real treat for me. Currently the museum is in the process of moving to the historic East Kong Yick Building. By the time you read this, the museum should be operating in high gear.

Wing Luke made an indelible mark on the Asian community, on Seattle, and on Washington State. Luke was a high-achieving student, was awarded a Bronze Star during his U.S. Army service in World War II, and was appointed Washington's Assistant State Attorney General. In 1962 Luke was sworn in as a member of the Seattle City Council, becoming the first American of Asian decent to be elected to office in the Pacific Northwest. Tragically, he died in a plane crash in 1965 while returning from a fishing trip.

The Wing Luke Asian Museum is the nation's largest pan-Asian Pacific American museum and was selected as the Smithsonian Institution's first affiliate museum in the Pacific Northwest.

Wing Luke Asian Museum is located at 719 South King Street. For more information call (206) 623-5124 or visit www.wingluke.org.

It's Not the Great Wall, but It's Still Pretty Cool
Historic Chinatown West Gate

It's common in China as well as in Chinese communities in the United States to erect ornate entrance gates. Seattle's Chinatown is now counted among them. In early 2008 workers completed the Historic Chinatown West Gate, which straddles South King Street at Fifth Avenue South at the western border of the Chinatown–International District

You won't need a key to pass through this gate, just a smile and a great attitude.

★ ★

Sir Mix-a-Lot

Born Anthony Ray in Seattle on August 12, 1963, the rap artist known as Sir Mix-a-Lot has accomplished incredible success in a city little known for creating music in the rap genre. The Grammy Award–winning, platinum-selling recording artist is best known for his crossover mega-hit "Baby Got Back," a ditty dedicated to women possessing decidedly plump posteriors.

A remarkable aspect of Sir Mix-a-Lot's success is how much of it he accomplished virtually on his own. Intensely driven, the singer's achievements are largely due to his own efforts at recording, self-promotion, and a general never-give-up approach to life.

Sir Mix-a-Lot also has a reputation for working outside his own genre, specifically experimenting with fusing rap and grunge/metal, like his collaborations with such Seattle rock bands as Metal Church and Mudhoney. He also partnered with the Presidents of the United States of America in a band called Subset.

An interesting note: Apparently, many fans mistook the Broadway in his hit single "Posse on Broadway" for the one in New York. Well, if you visit http://maps.live.com/?v=2&cid=AAC4007787524E04!110, you'll find a map of Seattle that tracks Sir Mix-a-Lot's song by lyrics as he rolls through Seattle, eventually ending up on Broadway—Seattle's Broadway!

neighborhood. Plans are now in the works to erect its twin at the eastern end of Chinatown, at Eighth Avenue and South King Street.

It was amazing to track the transformation from the I-beam steel skeleton to the spectacular, vividly adorned gate. An endowment has been established to maintain the gate, which was painted using high-quality automotive paint. Protruding wires and a sound-emitting device have been installed to reduce the notorious effects of our feathered friends.

In the Seattle spirit of interactivity, with a bit of fund-raising pragmatism, folks who've donated to the project can have their names etched on bronze plaques, which will adorn a black-and-white granite slab imported from—where else—China. Categories run from the "Swan" level for at least $100 to the "Imperial Dragon" for those donating $100,000 or more.

The Historic Chinatown West Gate is located at Fifth Avenue South and South King Street.

Thanks, Sis
Kobe Terrace

Kobe Terrace Park, in the Chinatown–International District neighborhood, has a unique distinction: It was created in 1973 to honor Seattle's very first sister-city association, established on October 10, 1957 with Kobe, Japan.

With a population of almost 1.5 million, Kobe is Japan's seventh-largest city. It is a port city and the capital of Hyogo Prefecture on the island of Honshu. To celebrate the fortieth anniversary of the relationship, Kobe's mayor traveled with a delegation to take part in Seattle's Seafair events.

The citizens of Seattle, represented by Mayor Norm Rice, traveled to Kobe and presented its citizens with a statue of a sea otter and a Sequoia tree as a gift. The people of Kobe have been similarly generous, and the most notable gifts are on view in Kobe Terrace. Spectacular is the word for these gifts: Pine and cherry trees surround a 200-year-old stone lantern weighing an incredible four tons.

Kobe Terrace is located at 221 Sixth Avenue South. For more information call (206) 684-4075 or visit www.seattle.gov/parks/park_detail .asp?ID=3915.

Look closely at the photo and you may see a small superhero figure placed on the giant lantern in Kobe Terrace Park. I could have removed it for the photo, but who am I to decide on the suitability of someone's spiritual offering?

Nothing Funny about This One

Wah Mee Massacre

This curiosity is obviously one without humor; it was the single deadliest day in Seattle crime history. On February 18, 1983, three men entered the Wah Mee gambling club in Chinatown and bound, robbed, shot, and killed or left for dead fourteen human beings. All but one of their victims perished in the bloody slaughter. The lone survivor, Wai Chin, a sixty-two-year-old *pai gow* (Chinese domino game) dealer, testified against the vermin who invaded the club that night just before midnight.

★ ★

A twenty-two-year-old Chinese immigrant named Willie Mak had accrued a large gambling debt. Motivated to use crime to clear up his debts, he targeted the affluent Wah Mee. He recruited two accomplices, Benjamin Ng and Tony Ng (no relation).

The three men lashed the fourteen victims' hands and feet with nylon cords before using their guns to methodically execute them. After the gunmen fled, Wai Chin, who'd survived his wound, managed to free himself from his bonds and stumbled out of the club to seek help.

Mak and Benjamin Ng were captured by police within hours of the murders; Tony Ng hid out in Canada for two years before being arrested and extradited to the United States. Although the murders were a capital crime, Canada would only extradite Ng on the condition that he be spared the death penalty. Mak was initially sentenced to death, but his sentence was reduced to life without parole. The court also sentenced Benjamin Ng to a life sentence, although only for assault and robbery. He was found to have been under duress from Mak with regard to the murders.

Many years have passed since the massacre, but people no longer pass through the portals of the Wah Mee, whose doors in an alley paralleling Maynard Avenue South remain chained and padlocked. The club, which was a historic speakeasy during Prohibition and one of the highest stakes gambling clubs in the Pacific Northwest, lives on—or at least its ghost does—in that dark place within the minds of Seattleites where things hide that we'd rather forget, but never will.

Orient Yourself

Hing Hay Park

Few places within Seattle's urban core are more interesting than Hing Hay Park, in the heart of Chinatown. *Hing Hay* means "Park for Pleasurable Gatherings," and it is an apt description. Some folks practice Tai Chi Chuan, a Chinese martial art/exercise system of precise and fluid movement, while others simply sit and enjoy one another's company and conversation.

The Sad Story of Frances Farmer

Frances Farmer may be the truest Hollywood-era movie star to have called Seattle home. Over a lengthy, albeit undulating, career, she starred in movies with legends like Bing Crosby and Tyrone Power. A movie of her life was made in 1982 starring Jessica Lang, who was nominated for an Academy Award for her portrayal of Farmer.

Frances Farmer's story, which began with her birth on September 19, 1913, in Seattle, makes Britney Spears seem like a poster child for the Girl Scouts of America. From precocious student at West Seattle High School to A-list Hollywood starlet, she trod a wild path.

Farmer was arrested for drunk driving and assault (including throwing an inkwell at a judge), confined to mental institutions, and worked as a receptionist. She eventually resumed her film and stage career and had a successful TV show, but until cancer took her, she continued to search for, but never quite captured, that elusive peace for which she seemed to yearn.

Reportedly, Nirvana's Kurt Cobain thought portions of his life mirrored Farmer's. In fact, Cobain wrote a song entitled "Frances Farmer Will Have Her Revenge on Seattle." I'm not sure for what she requires revenge on Seattle, but I suppose we will never know. Sadly, Kurt joined Frances in 1994.

If you're the type who likes to immerse yourself in foreign culture but don't have the time or financial wherewithal to purchase an extended vacation to China, Japan, or Korea, then Seattle is the cultural transporter for you. Sit and enjoy the view and warmth of Asian art and culture without leaving Seattle.

Hing Hay Park, a lot of park in such a small space, was purchased in 1970 with funds from the Forward Thrust bond propositions. Designed by landscape architect S. K. Sakuma, the park is dominated by the ornate Grand Pavilion, which was actually designed and constructed in Taiwan before being transported to Seattle for installation in 1974.

Hing Hay Park is located at 423 Maynard Avenue South. For more information call (206) 684-4075 or visit www.seattle.gov/parks/park_detail.asp?ID=358.

Here's My View

Kerry Park

Kerry Park is one of the first parks I visited after arriving in Seattle. Friends told me it offered the best view of Seattle in Seattle, and I wasn't disappointed. Unlike a view of a city that changes only over years with the addition and subtraction of various buildings, spectacular though it may be, this view from Kerry Park—encompassing Downtown, the Space Needle, Elliott Bay, West Seattle, Bainbridge Island, and Mount Rainier—changes with the moment.

On some days you can see Mount Rainier painted on a clear blue canvass; on other days you may only see Mount Rainier when it peeks out between puffs of billowing clouds. Elliott Bay reflects the sky's ever-changing moods. Ferryboats, pleasure craft, commercial vessels, and U.S. Navy ships crisscross the waves as they continually change the seascape, heading into and out of the Port of Seattle.

What can be even more fun is to watch people as they enjoy this 1.5-acre park, not only for its unparalleled view but also for its own lazy position, reclining on this nook on the south flank of Queen Anne Hill. I'm sure you will also enjoy Doris Chase's 15-foot-tall sculpture *Changing Form,* which was added to the park in 1971 as a gift from the Kerrys' children. A plaque mounted on a wall states the purpose of the park simply and eloquently; it reads: "Kerry Park given to the City

★ ★

in 1927 by Mr. and Mrs. Albert Sperry Kerry Sr. so that all who stop here may enjoy this view."

Kerry Park is located at 211 West Highland Drive. For more information call (206) 684-4075.

The view from Kerry Park is definitely one of the best of the Emerald City.

Get Yourself Some Cheap Sunglasses

Seattle sells more pairs of sunglasses per capita than any other American city. You don't believe me? Well, it's true, and I have empirical evidence to back the assertion. A mysterious black hole sucks in too many pairs to count during those long intervals between the sun's visits.

Here's how the phenomenon works. Residents of Honolulu or San Diego always have their shades with them. However, in Seattle, where sun sightings are rarer than those of Sasquatch, residents take their glasses off and toss them—somewhere. The next time the sun appears, they forget where the heck they put the darn things, so back to the sunglasses shop they go. So if you're a sunglasses entrepreneur, counterintuitive as it may seem, Seattle isn't such a bad place to set up shop.

One of those counterintuitive things in life: Seattle sells more sunglasses per capita than any other city in America—because we lose them during those long gaps between sunny days.

3

East

I think the word diversity *is way overused these days. However, there's no other word that better describes this part of Seattle. Having worked in the East Precinct for so long, it's the part of the city I know best.*

Seattle's east neighborhoods are dotted with many historic—and perhaps hysteric—features. Inside Volunteer Park alone there are several historic sites surrounded by pastoral lawns bordered by a beautiful assortment of trees, shrubs, and flower gardens. There's the flora-filled conservatory, the Seattle Asian Art Museum, a clinker-brick water tower, a reservoir, tennis courts, a statue of William Seward, an amphitheater, a kiddie pool, and the Black Sun *sculpture through which you'll catch a unique view of the Space Needle—if it's not cloudy, that is.*

Just over the fence in Lake View Cemetery, many Seattle pioneers such as Arthur Denny, Henry Yesler, and Doc Maynard are laid to rest. You'll also find Bruce and Brandon Lee. There are even a few Confederate veterans, buried at the foot of an impressive granite memorial erected by the Daughters of the Confederacy (yes, right here in Seattle). Across the street, appropriately to the north, is the Grand Army of the Republic cemetery, where hundreds of Union veterans are buried.

All this and we haven't even touched colorful Broadway, the edgy Central District, or snooty (with affection) Madison Park. My advice: Go east young man, or woman.

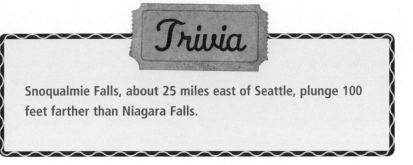

Snoqualmie Falls, about 25 miles east of Seattle, plunge 100 feet farther than Niagara Falls.

A Bit of Everything—Even If You Don't Want It

Capitol Hill

Before it became Capitol Hill, it had been known as Broadway Hill. Although folks can't seem to agree on how the neighborhood originally got its name, in the 1950s it was known as Catholic Hill in addition to Broadway Hill due to the area's heavy Roman Catholic population. The neighborhood is bounded by Route 520 and Interlaken Park to the north, East Pike and East Madison Streets to the south, Twenty-third and Twenty-fourth Avenues to the east, and Interstate 5 to the west. Putting emphasis on the hill, the area claims half of Seattle's dozen steepest hills, with grades from 18 to 21 percent slicing down its eastern and western slopes.

There are two stories involving the same person as to how Capitol Hill got its name. Some say James Moore, who platted much of this area of the city, gave it the name hoping he could lure Washington's state capital from Olympia to Seattle. Another story posits that Moore named it for his wife's home neighborhood in Denver. It seems the consensus is a combination of the two. For harmony's sake, let's go with that.

Capitol Hill is probably the most dynamic and definitely the most diversified neighborhood in Seattle. The center of Seattle's gay community, it also contains the clubs that first fostered grunge music, churches, institutions of higher education, retail establishments, a

Little Dragon

Bruce Lee, an influential role model as I grew up, was a big reason for my interest in the city of Seattle. Growing up, I was a Bruce Lee fanatic.

There's nothing I can mention about Bruce Lee that hasn't been covered hundreds or even thousands of times around the world. However, I do have some personal observations. Bruce Lee was born in San Francisco to Chinese parents visiting from Hong Kong with a traveling theater group. He moved to Seattle as a young man, attended the University of Washington, started his first martial arts schools, and, sadly, has his final resting place here.

More tourists have asked me for directions to Bruce Lee's gravesite than to any other attraction. As tourists approach, I rattle off directions before they ask; I know the look. On one occasion, while at Bruce Lee's gravesite a young Asian woman and a man with a motion picture camera approached and asked to interview me. They were filming a documentary about Bruce Lee for broadcast in China. She asked me a few questions and, me being such a big fan, probably got more than she'd bargained for.

When I got home I told my wife the story and said, "Hey, I'll be famous in China." She replied, "You'll be famous on some Chinese film editor's floor."

Ouch!

Bruce Lee is interred in Plot #276 at Lake View Cemetery, 1554 15th Avenue East. For more information on Bruce Lee, visit www .bruceleefoundation.com.

Ferrari dealer, restaurants, and residences. Its densely populated neighborhoods, the second most dense in the city, contain all manner of homes, from charming apartment buildings containing simple single-occupancy flats, to modest single family homes, to the most magnificent historic mansions in the city. It also boasts (or laments, depending on whether you're buying or selling) Seattle's highest home values.

Another Capitol Hill magnet is its claim to historic attractions. Lake View Cemetery is the final resting place of most of Seattle's founding pioneers such as the Dennys, Borens, and Yeslers. There's Volunteer Park, Cal Anderson Park, the Grand Army of the Republic Cemetery, Bruce Lee's gravesite, and much more. These features add flavor to an already savory goulash that makes The Hill a great place to live, work, or simply wander around on a nice sunny, or for that matter rainy, day.

Capitol Hill is located in east-central Seattle.

Weird? Well, It's Supposed to Be

Seattle Museum of the Mysteries

Many American cities boast a history of mysteries. Seattle is no different, and with preeminent mysteries such as Bigfoot right in its backyard, it's no mystery that this is home to the Seattle Museum of the Mysteries, Washington's only museum of paranormal culture.

This isn't simply a place where you can see a collection of dusty, blurry photographs of Sasquatch, crop circles, and various Seattle ghosts. This museum is incredibly diverse in its exhibits as well as its participatory programs.

The museum offers a ninety-minute ghost-hunting jaunt along the sidewalks of Capitol Hill on Saturdays at 5:00 and 7:00 p.m. For the truly brave, or foolish, from 10:00 p.m. to midnight the museum hosts a "Lock-In" at the museum, billed as being "located within one of the most haunted buildings in Seattle." According to the folks at the museum, their resident ghost bears a haunting resemblance to Nikola Tesla.

A Pink Toe Truck?

I'd heard about Lincoln tow trucks at some point after I'd arrived in Seattle, as they have been one of the preeminent tow companies in the city. In fact, they've been contracted for police impounds for many years. However, Lincoln decided to play a little phonetic word game and built a honest-to-goodness "toe truck."

It's not enough that it's a tow truck with five little piggies riding above the cab; it's also painted bright pink. The tow, or toe, truck has been a parade favorite for years. However, I'd seen it most often at its longtime location at the Lincoln tow lot (or is that toe lot?) at Fairview and Mercer.

The truck was there for about twenty-five years until the owners sold the company and retired. If you'd like to see the toe truck up close and personal these days, you'll need to haul your butt down to the Museum of History & Industry.

The Museum of History & Industry (MOHAI) is located in McCurdy Park at 2700 24th Avenue East. For more information call (206) 324-1126 or visit www.seattlehistory.org.

Whether you need a toe or a tow, this pink car's conveyor will foot the bill. Courtesy MOHAI

I know what you're thinking: *I'm not one of those who'd be afraid. That sounds like silly nonsense.* Okay, that's fine—but don't come running to me when you dash screaming out of the building, freaking out the freaks on Broadway and leaving only a hole with your shape in the front door of the museum.

Seattle Museum of the Mysteries is located at 623 Broadway East. For more information call (206) 328-6499 or visit www.seattlechatclub .org/museum.html.

Bums and Baseball and Other Stuff, Too

Cal Anderson Park

This park, named for Cal Anderson, the first openly gay member of the Washington State legislature, recently surprised me—and that's saying something, since I've been working in this area for so long. I'd never truly appreciated it until recently. Over the past several years the park

Capping a century-old reservoir with artworks, lawns, paths, and sports fields created a great place to play.

No, the Toilet Paper's Not Made of Gold

It may have been a good idea on paper, but as it turns out, that must've been toilet paper. When state-of-the-art equipment meets urban reality, you may wind up with a seriously smelly situation.

Citizens, merchants in particular, had long complained that Seattle had no public restrooms. This forced people to use commercial restrooms, much to the consternation of storeowners who felt compelled to restrict their facilities to customer use. This, in turn, required people to either become a "customer" by making an unnecessary purchase, "holding it" until they made it home, or peeing in an alley.

In an attempt to solve this problem, the city council, overriding the mayor's veto, approved funding for seven automated, self-cleaning, space-age public toilets. "What about the cost?" some people wondered. "What about drug use?" "What about prostitution?" Citizens brought their concerns to the council's attention. But forget about using facts to hobble something supported by an enlightened, progressive city council—the spaceship-looking lavatories had landed.

has undergone a dramatic transformation. What was once the venerable, albeit bland, Lincoln Reservoir (constructed between 1889 and 1901) surrounded by sparse vegetation, drooling drunks, and lazy bums has emerged as a jewel on Capitol Hill.

Today the park is quite attractive with its wending paths, flowing lawns, and vibrant flowerbeds. Among these amenities you'll find some

The restrooms had become havens for heroin hypes and toilets for trollops tramping their trade. Calls for outdoor feces cleanups actually increased significantly after the toilets' installation.

Why, you ask? For one thing, the user is allowed fifteen minutes before the door automatically opens, and any drug dealer or "business" lady within will likely use every one of those minutes. Next, after use the door seals and the unit self-cleans for another ten minutes. I don't know about you, but I'm not going to wait twenty-five minutes; I'm gonna find other options.

Councilman Richard Conlin voted in favor of the toilets but now says, "They haven't worked out the way we'd hoped. . . . We're going to have to go back to the drawing board. They've become dens of illegal behavior." In a later interview he added that "high-tech public toilets are not as reliable as someone who really needs a restroom would hope . . . a little observation showed that plenty of people couldn't get the computerized lock to open with their quarters. Other people have had the opposite problem. A bus driver told the newspaper the doors opened on one of his passengers just as she was pulling up her pants."

Thankfully, the automated public toilets are no longer in Seattle.

of the coolest water features to be found in an urban park. There's a pleasing sense of flow as a volcano-like cone rising from the north end gushes water down its sides like crystal-clear lava. From its base the water streams down a narrow culvert that opens into a larger pool and flows around fixed stone protrusions, creating a fascinating texture and sound to the water.

Adjacent to the park is one of the most attractive public sports parks located near Seattle's urban center. The Bobby Morris Playfield accommodates athletes who enjoy playing soccer, baseball, softball, and tennis. All in all, the folks involved in this project did it right on this one. Whether you're out for a vigorous game of tennis or a lazy picnic on a grassy knoll, want to sit on a bench and play your guitar or sketch the waterfall sculpture, you won't find a single better place to do it all.

Cal Anderson Park is located at 1635 11th Avenue. For more information call (206) 684-4057 or visit www.seattle.gov/parks/park_detail .asp?ID=3102.

Talk about History—Okay, Let's
Seattle University

Seattle University, a Jesuit institution, is remarkable in so many ways that it's difficult to select only a few tidbits within this short tease—but we'll see what we can do. Incidentally, I collected many fond memories as a supervisor for the university's public safety department before becoming a Seattle police officer.

Several university buildings are steeped in Seattle history, or so beautifully constructed that they draw people on their own intrinsic merits. For example, the Garrand Building's history is unparalleled on campus.

The marvelous 1890s brick-and-stone building, named for one of Seattle U's founders, Father Victor Garrand, initially served as the entire Seattle College campus. As century-old buildings tend to be, it

Trivia

The only NBA basketball game to be called off due to rain was in Seattle on January 5, 1986.

Changing the World —Big Time

Although its chief corporate campus is located across Lake Washington from Seattle in the serene suburb of Redmond, Microsoft does have facilities in Seattle, and the software giant is most definitely associated around the world with the Emerald City. After all, company founder Bill Gates was born in Seattle.

The fact that I'm writing this entry using Microsoft Word stands as a testament to the influence of the company on daily life. And while they've had a major impact on the world, I don't know anyone in the Seattle area who doesn't know someone who either works for or has worked for Microsoft at some point in the past.

It might surprise you to know that Microsoft offers something that has little to do with the computer stuff that has made the company world renowned. It's also not something you can buy at the computer store; you can only find it at Microsoft's headquarters. At Microsoft's Redmond campus, a few minutes east of Seattle, you can take a tour of the Microsoft Art Collection. Yes, the software supercompany has a very impressive collection of artworks, and it invites you to take a peek.

Microsoft believes that this exhibit serves several purposes. For employees, the artworks provide inspiration and spark creativity. For business guests, the collection shows off Microsoft's expansive personality. And finally, it allows the company to put forth a unique and popular public-relations effort.

You can call for an appointment to take a tour or visit on Thursday, when tours are open and available for registration on a first-come, first-served basis. Programs are free, but Microsoft requests that you RSVP to artevent@microsoft.com within two weeks of your visit—so plan ahead.

qualified as what historians call "one scary place." One spooky night I was patrolling outside Garrand. The university's science labs had been housed there many years ago, and the building still held some items from that era—including, it was rumored, at least one mummified body. That image stuck.

The last check was the window at the top of a rickety fire escape. I screwed up my gumption and climbed the creaking metal structure. When I poked my head up over the top step to the landing, my heart leapt into my throat. Staring back into my flashlight beam were five pairs of glowing eyes—mummies! Resisting the urge to launch myself off the railing, I regained my composure. It wasn't a horde of the undead behind those eyes but a family of raccoons often seen prowling the campus. I'd wondered where those furry bandits had disappeared to. And, yes, these raccoons were smack in the middle of the big city.

On a less-scary front, bet you didn't know there was a time when lil' ol' Seattle University had one of the best NCAA Division I men's basketball teams in the nation. On eleven occasions between 1953 and 1969, the Chieftains (since renamed the Redhawks) reached the NCAA Division I Tournament. Behind Elgin Baylor, the 1958 Chieftains earned a coveted spot in the National Championship final. Unfortunately Seattle University lost to the University of Kentucky 84–72. Seattle U eventually left Division I and has been playing at the Division II level. The university hopes to regain Division I status by 2010.

Seattle University is located at 901 12th Avenue. For more information call (206) 296-6000 or visit www.seattleu.edu.

Trivia

The largest wireless (Wi-Fi) network in the world is at Microsoft's corporate headquarters campus.

Another Seattle First
Tashkent Park

Tashkent Park, located a few blocks west of Broadway, occupies only about a half acre of land in the midst of an urban residential neighborhood; apartments rise all around. It may be small, but it's important in that it has a "first" distinction: Not only is it a first for Seattle, but it's also a first for America. Tashkent Park was named for Tashkent, Uzbekistan (then a part of the USSR). Participants in the United States' Sister City Association, in 1973 Seattle and Tashkent became the first sister cities between America and the then-Soviet Union.

Ann Rules!

This is a very special entry for me for two reasons. First because Ann and I have something in common, and I'm not just talking about writing; Ann was also a Seattle police officer. The second reason is that this generous woman took the time from her extremely busy schedule to read my first book and provided a quote that still reddens my face to read it, a blurb we happily used on the front cover.

For a couple of you way in the back there who may not have heard of Ann Rule, she has established herself as the world's preeminent true-crime writer and the standard in the genre. Over three decades she's written and published twenty books and more than 1,400 articles.

Ann has a gift for writing her nonfiction in a way that novels capture the imagination—absolutely riveting the readers to the page. Ann is a true Seattle treasure.

The city park that honors this association is quaint, with a beautiful sculpture; rolling, grassy mounds; and a covered picnic area. However, as with too many urban parks, scan the area carefully before you spend any time there. The park's quaint charms attract not only good citizens and tourists but also derelicts, druggies, and other undesirable denizens.

Tashkent Park is located at 511 Boylston Avenue East. For more information call (206) 684-4075 or visit www.seattle.gov/parks/park_detail.asp?ID=384.

Nellie Finds Her Niche
Cornish College of the Arts

My wife, who'd spent much of her youth in gymnastics and dance classes before using the fitness she acquired to fight fires, applied to Cornish many (many, shhh!) years ago to pursue her love of dance. I can't describe the disappointment I saw in her face when she read the rejection letter. However, try to imagine how great her disappointment was when I came across that letter a couple of years later and realized she'd misunderstood the wording. She hadn't been denied; she'd been accepted, conditioned upon taking a specific prerequisite class. Doh!

This story is a personal experience about a unique and special school in which alumni, faculty, and the city of Seattle take much pride. Piano and voice teacher and arts visionary Nellie Centennial Cornish (1876–1956), whose middle name honors the year of her birth, founded the Cornish School in 1914 in a building at Broadway Avenue and Pine Street. The school was instantly popular, enrolling 600 students within its first three years.

The Cornish College of the Arts, as it is now formally known, is one of the very few arts schools in the nation fully accredited to offer a bachelor of fine arts degree in dance, design, fine arts, and theater, as well as a bachelor of music degree. Cornish boasts the lowest student-to-teacher ratio of any arts school in America.

Cornish has a list of renowned past faculty and students who went on to make from significant to stellar contributions to the arts, broadcast, and entertainment worlds—among them the enormously gifted Ann Wilson, lead singer of Seattle's legendary rock group Heart; talented actor Brendan Fraser; and network news pioneer Chet Huntley.

Cornish College of the Arts is located at 1000 Lenora Street. For more information call (206) 726-5016 or (800) 726-ARTS (2787) or visit www.cornish.edu.

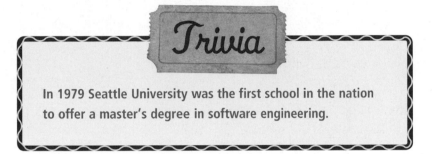

Trivia

In 1979 Seattle University was the first school in the nation to offer a master's degree in software engineering.

Care to Tango?
Broadway Dance Steps

On Capitol Hill's inimitable Broadway, you may be a bit puzzled as you stroll along and up ahead see seemingly sane and even sober people suddenly break into dance. Beware. As those folks collect their sanity and mosey on and you near the spot that so afflicted them, you may find yourself suddenly busting your own moves as bronze footprints embedded into the sidewalk tickle your tootsies to tango.

One person's art is another person's perplexed expression or, in some instances, condescending snicker. However, whether or not folks realize that Jack Mackie's *Broadway Dance Steps* is indeed art seems way beside the point. Over the past three decades we can only imagine the number of people who've enjoyed following the dance steps, which are organized into a series of numbered male and female shoeprints set to the rumba, tango, fox-trot, and, as of January 2007, the cha-cha.

★ ★

No one can resist the temptation to toe tap or two-step when his or her feet hit these feet. Heather Pomper

In an interview in 2006, Mackie said he intended the final element of his artwork to be the interaction between viewer and art. The artwork sits inanimate in the sidewalk until a passing pedestrian, upon seeing the festive footprints, is moved to boogie—in a sense, imbuing the steps with animation. Almost as fun as tracing the dance steps yourself is watching other people, especially tourists, as they encounter the bronze footprints, which you'd swear are magnetic the way people's feet are irresistibly drawn to them.

The *Broadway Dance Steps* run along the sidewalk on the east side of the 400 block of Broadway across from the Broadway Market.

The Blue
G.A.R. Cemetery

While exploring the north end of the Capitol Hill neighborhood, you might make a wrong turn and stumble upon a modest, unassuming patch of land surrounded by a thick hedge and dominated by a massive stone monument at its center. The granite monolith is surrounded by hundreds of small, weatherworn headstones.

Buried adjacent a place as mundane, and modern, as an off-leash dog park complete with a dog-poop-baggie dispenser are more than 200 Civil War Army and Navy veterans of the Union Forces of the United States along with their wives.

You've discovered Seattle's Grand Army of the Republic (G.A.R.) Cemetery. The G.A.R. was a fraternal organization formed after the Civil War to support Union war veterans. First platted in 1896, the 2.3-acre plot is the only municipally maintained Civil War cemetery in the United States. Together, the Friends of the G.A.R. Cemetery Park and the Seattle Parks Department maintain this sacred ground, which contains so much history of patriotic sacrifice and civic contribution.

I find it heartening that nearly a century and a half after these soldiers and sailors sacrificed for their country, they are still honored every Memorial Day when volunteers place tiny American flags at each veteran's grave.

Wishing to put the war behind them, many veterans found their way across a vast, expanding, and reunited America, ready to resume their lives and work for their version of the American dream, this time in Seattle.

It's awe inspiring to roam the park in solemn reflection and meet its permanent inhabitants. Some men, born in foreign lands such as Ireland, England, Germany, Canada, and Sweden, had loyally served their adopted country. The veterans, officers and enlisted men, represent many military units from several states, including Ohio, Vermont, and Maine. Also interred here are sailors from New York, Pennsylvania, and New Hampshire who served aboard Union naval vessels. You'll even find a half dozen soldiers from assorted U.S. Colored Infantry Regiments. Black and white soldiers may have been segregated in the Army, but in death they are buried side by side.

★ ★

Grand Army of the Republic Cemetery is located on the 1200 block
of East Howe Street, just north of Lake View Cemetery. For more information send an e-mail to friends@fgar.org or visit www.fgar.org.

The Gray

Confederate Memorial

Perhaps even more surprising than finding a Union Army Veteran's
cemetery in Seattle, thousands of miles from the nearest Civil War
battlefield, is what you'll find about 2 blocks south on 15th Avenue
East. Within the Gothic iron entrance gates of the venerable Lake
View Cemetery, you'll find one of the last things you'd expect to find
in Seattle—outside of a severe case of sunstroke: an immense, twin-
columned Georgian granite memorial to Confederate veterans.

Not something I'd ever expected to find in the great Pacific Northwest, the memorial to veterans of the Southern Army was erected and

Yes, there's a Confederate Civil War memorial in Seattle.
Veterans of the Southern Army rest beneath this Georgian
granite monument.

dedicated by the Daughters of the Confederacy, Robert E. Lee Chapter, in 1926. The stone structure stands sentinel over the graves of seven Confederate officers and soldiers.

Marjorie Ann Reeves of the Daughters of the Confederacy says the existence of a memorial to Confederate veterans in Seattle shouldn't surprise us. She explains that after the war, many veterans from both the North and South traveled west to places such as Seattle to put the war behind them and start new lives.

Ms. Reeves says that contrary to the animosity and old grudges one might expect, former soldiers of the C.S.A. (Confederate States of America) adapted to life in Seattle and contributed significantly to the young city's early growth as an emerging seaport and timber hub.

Sadly, the monument was desecrated in 2003 when brass plaques and crossed rifles were pried from their positions and stolen. Some believe the theft was politically motivated, perpetrated by those opposed to the presence of a memorial to the Confederacy in Seattle. Others believe the items were stolen for their value as historic arti-facts. Still others believe the brass objects were stolen simply for their value as recycled metal. Whatever the reason, this was a terrible crime against Seattle's authentic history, and all Seattleites are poorer for it.

Some might say it's at best ironic and at worst sacrilegious that veterans from opposing sides of the War between the States (or, if you Southerners prefer, the War of Northern Aggression) are buried as close to one another as the skirmish lines from where they once fought. For me, it seems fitting that although enemies as young men, they eventually came together in Seattle and joined to help the city grow into what would become a world-class American city. And now veterans from both North and South lie for eternity only a few hundred yards apart in the center of their adopted city, thousands of miles from the battlefields that wrested from each of them a great measure of sacrifice.

The Confederate Memorial is located in Lake View Cemetery, 1554 15th Avenue East. (Bear right at first fork; the monument is on your right.) For more information visit www.seattleudc.org.

Hey, The Mountain's Out!

One of the most curious things about Seattle involves something that isn't even technically within the city limits. However, it's as much a part of the city as Seattle's Space Needle or waterfront. It's Mount Rainier or, as locals call it, The Mountain.

I'd only been in Seattle a short time and was involved in a conversation when my friend suddenly said, "The Mountain's out," and then continued the conversation.

I looked to where he'd unconsciously pointed, and there she was— Mount Rainier (or Tahoma, as this area's first residents called her) rising from the horizon in majestic hues of blue and white, a few wispy clouds cavorting at the summit.

Seattle culture is imbued with this curious verbal affectation, and it wasn't very long before my own vernacular was similarly affected. Today I repeat the same phrase without thought of its quirkiness. "The Mountain's out," I'll say. Out-of-state folks look at me as strangely and ask, "Where else would it be?"

As with the sun, the phrase is a function of our clouds. There are so many overcast days in Seattle that it's nearly a phenomenon when you can actually see Mount Rainier. One thing this does for Seattleites is help to maintain the mountain's fresh appeal. On each rare day, when the gods paint the southeast sky cerulean and Mount Rainier stands so crystal clear, you feel you could reach out and scoop snow from its slopes. Your eyes are reborn and you realize that as long as you live in Seattle, you'll never tire of the awesome site of The Mountain—when it's out.

A Park with Many Faces

Volunteer Park

Although Volunteer Park is home to many Seattle curiosities, some of which you'll find elsewhere in this book, the park itself is a curiosity in its own right. In 1876 the city purchased forty acres of land in the center of what is now known as Capitol Hill for $2,000 from sawmill operator J. M. Colman.

The "park" existed as a municipal parcel of land without any express purpose until 1885, when a city ordinance designated it as a cemetery. After only two years in this capacity, interred bodies were ordered removed, and the parcel became a city park. Talk about a make-up-your-mind-damn-it moment for the gravediggers.

The park's name was changed again, this time to Lake View Park, and adjacent land that had been a part of the park became Lake View Cemetery. In 1901 the park's name was changed once again, and perhaps for good, to Volunteer Park in honor of Spanish-American War veterans.

By 1893 timber had been cleared, making room for a greenhouse facility. Over the next several years, flowerbeds, lawns, paths, picnic tables, and kids' swings were added along with a high-pressure reservoir. Between 1904 and 1909 the famous Olmstead Brothers of Boston provided plans for formal gardens, a system of drives, water features such as lily ponds and a wading pool, a music pavilion, and a conservatory, all of which were completed by 1912.

Today there are too many activities in Volunteer Park to mention them all. Here are a few stars: the Seattle Asian Art Museum, conservatory, water tower, statue of William Seward (the dude who bought Alaska), *Black Sun* sculpture, and don't forget the free concerts at the amphitheater and the Shakespeare in the Park performances. The park also boasts wide-open, grassy fields perfect for a game of flag or Frisbee football, rugby, or, for the brave of heart, taking a crack at getting a Seattle tan on a rare sunny day.

★ ★

Volunteer Park is located at 1247 15th Avenue East. For more information call (206) 684-4075 or visit www.seattle.gov/parks/park_detail.asp?ID=399.

Plants in Glass Houses Shouldn't Throw—Smells
Volunteer Park Conservatory

Ghostly elegance described the conservatory the day I saw it swathed in an early-morning Seattle mist. Based on London's Crystal Palace, the Victorian-style greenhouse, completed in 1912, sits at the northeast portion of the park. It serves as a backdrop for the statue of William

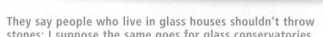

They say people who live in glass houses shouldn't throw stones; I suppose the same goes for glass conservatories.

★ ★

H. Seward (1801–1872), which stands at the intersection of three park roads. Seward was Lincoln's secretary of state and the man behind the purchase of Alaska from Russia.

I have to admit that every time I see the conservatory I'm reminded of the movie *Disclosure* (Michael Douglas, Demi Moore), in which a shot of an event at the conservatory, which is in Volunteer Park, is misidentified as the Washington Park Arboretum, located a mile or so to the east.

The conservatory is divided into five houses, each with its own subclimate or sub-subclimate. In this verdant wonderland you'll find a cactus house, a fern house, a palm house, a bromeliad house, and a house specifically for seasonal displays. The conservatory is also known for its display of the infamous corpse flower (*Amorphophallus titanium*), borrowed from the University of Washington's Botany Greenhouse and known for its horrendous stench when in rare bloom.

The conservatory is the anchor of the Seattle Parks and Recreation's horticultural center, where plants are nurtured for use in parks around the city. The facility is also used as a repository for plants confiscated by the U.S. Fish and Wildlife Service.

A visit to the conservatory is a sure hit for Northwest natives as well as for your out-of-town guests. The staff is friendly and knowledgeable. The orchid display is remarkable, and the sheer size of some of the cacti will prickle you into wide-eyed fascination.

The straightest way to the conservatory is to enter Volunteer Park at the entrance off 15th Avenue East and East Galer Street. One note, though: Don't take the same route when you leave—it's a one-way road.

The Volunteer Park Conservatory is located at 1400 East Galer Street. For more information call (206) 684-4743 or visit www.seattle.gov/parks/parkspaces/VolunteerPark/conservatory.htm.

Clinker Bricks?

Volunteer Park Water Tower

Volunteer Park's enchanting water tower and observatory is a true Seattle treasure swiped straight out of an Old Country fairytale. Built in 1906, the tower appears to rise out of a 20-foot mound, thick with verdant shrubbery and surrounded by a roundabout road at the 14th

This still-functioning 1906 water tower is one of the most intriguing structures in Seattle.

★ ★

Avenue East and East Prospect Street entrance. The tower's construction alone—it was built of clinker bricks—is enough to captivate the imagination.

If you're wondering what the heck clinker bricks are, basically they're bricks that were "overcooked" in the kiln, which changed their surface texture and color, pocking, warping, and purpling the bricks. They're heavier than most bricks and "clink" rather than "clack" when knocked together. The blemished bricks enhance the structure's beauty, cloaking it in a medieval-tinged shroud.

Jacketed in a 100-foot-tall brick cylinder, the 883,000-gallon, copper-capped holding tank has an observation deck offering 360-degree views. Through several arched windows, the observatory provides an intimate view of the Space Needle and the Olympic Mountains.

Affixed along the interior wall of the observatory are several attractive plaques displaying the lively stories of Seattle Park's rich history and legacy.

Is the view worth the climb? You bet it is—but you'd best be ready for it. There is no elevator, just 106 metal steps winding up a relatively narrow spiral staircase to the observatory. I'm not saying you need be fit enough to summit Mount Rainier, but a reasonable level of fitness is advised. If you have time on your hands, you can allocate a generous amount of time per step, ascending at your leisure. Besides, there are actually two stairways (one on the north and one on the south), so any impatient blokes can use the other stairs.

The water tower is located in Volunteer Park at 14th Avenue East and East Prospect Street. For more information call (206) 684-4075.

The Museum That Whispers
Seattle Asian Art Museum

The very first thing that strikes you about this museum is the building. It's smack in the middle of a city park, but somehow it fits. The art deco design lends itself perfectly to the park. This structure doesn't shout, "Look at me; here I am!" As large as it is, it whispers, "Pssst, I'm over here; come on in."

★ ★

I first set foot in this building back in the early 1980s, when it was home to the Seattle Art Museum (SAM). I still remember the featured exhibit at that time, a testament to SAM's impressive ability to draw folks through its doors. That exhibit was called "Arms & Armor," and on display was a collection of medieval European—well, arms and armor.

When SAM moved its main collection to downtown Seattle in 1991, work began on this building as the Seattle Asian Art Museum (SAAM). The SAAM's exhibits showcase the art of the Asian world. For example, showing at the time of this writing is "Inspired Simplicity: Contemporary Art from Korea and Chinese Art: A Seattle Perspective."

But wait . . . there's more. How about some freebies? Admission is free on the first Thursday of the month—for everyone. On the first Friday of the month seniors (age sixty-two and older) can slide in without paying. Still want more? Sure you do. Families can visit the museum for free on the first Saturday of each month.

The Seattle Asian Art Museum is located in Volunteer Park at 1400 East Prospect Street. For more information call (206) 654-3206 or visit www.seattleartmuseum.org/visit/visitSAAM.asp.

The Holy Box
St. Mark's Cathedral

William Shakespeare once said, "Timing is everything." The Bard could have been referring to the inauspicious beginnings of St. Mark's Episcopal Cathedral. Its original, spectacular design had to be scaled back because of the timing. Although fund-raising had begun in 1926 and continued through the pouring of the foundation in 1928, you know what followed the next year: the stock market crash of 1929. This financial crisis strapped many would-be donors to the construction effort.

Despite the donation drought, the cathedral was built and dedicated on Saturday, April 25, 1931. Due to the sparseness of the interior, the church was lovingly nicknamed the "Holy Box." At this time, the church still owed a quarter of a million dollars to bankers. For the next decade, the parish struggled to maintain the facility, but bankers were forced to foreclose on the cathedral. (Man, I would not have wanted to be one of those guys arriving at the pearly gates after that.)

While the cathedral remained closed from 1941 to 1943, an artillery unit of the U.S. Army leased and occupied the building for a year. In 1944 the church renegotiated the loan and the building reopened, once again as a place of worship. (Okay, so perhaps there was a reprieve for the bankers meeting Saint Peter.) A massive fund-raising effort was put forth, and in 1947, the church having finally paid off the debt, the mortgage was burned at the alter on Palm Sunday. In fact, the bankers paid the last $5,000. (All right, looks like they're off the hook.)

Over the years the cathedral has been renovated for various reasons, including replacing an aging pipe organ with the palatine, and world-renowned, Flentrop Pipe Organ. Folks often visit St. Mark's exclusively to see and to hear this stunning instrument.

St. Mark's occupies an interesting location. As you're driving north or south on Interstate 5, the cathedral appears to rise out of the densely wooded west slope of north Capitol Hill. On a personal note, when my daughter Heather was five years old, she shuffled down the aisle of St. Mark's, a pretty basket of flowers clutched in her little hands, as flower girl at her godmother's wedding.

St. Mark's Cathedral is located at 1245 10th Avenue East. For more information call (206) 323-0300 or visit www.saintmarks.org.

Carved in Stone

Black Sun

This is one of my favorite pieces of art, of any medium, in Seattle. Situated prominently in Volunteer Park on Capitol Hill, the *Black Sun* sculpture (1960–63) was a creation of artist Isamu Noguchi (1904–1988). At first glance this sculpture resembles a shiny black, oblong doughnut, its edges nibbled by some giant rodents. On second, third, or eighty-seventh glance, one sees that it's so much more.

★ ★

The *Black Sun* sculpture is named for the kind of sun
we see most in Seattle.

The sculpture is on my list of favorites, not only for its imagination-
captivating appearance—carved from black tamba granite—but also
for its precise location. Standing with your back to the Asian Art
Museum, peering through the center hole of the *Black Sun* and across
the shimmering waters of the reservoir, you get a spectacular view of
the Space Needle, Puget Sound, and on to the Olympic Mountains and
beyond, framed by the *Black Sun*'s mystical portal.

You'd be hard-pressed to find a more unique view of the Space
Needle than this one. The *Black Sun* is also one of Seattle's more
"interactive" pieces of art, evinced by the apparent compulsion of both
children and adults to clamber on, over, and through it—or to simply
caress its smooth, inviting surface.

The stone disk is set on edge upon a broad apron, inviting sunset
enthusiasts to gaze through it into the distance at a morphing, pan-
oramic commingling of brilliant cobalt and fiery hues. Oh, and one
more thing: DO NOT FORGET YOUR CAMERA!

* *

Black Sun is located in Volunteer Park at 14th Avenue East and East Prospect Street. For more information call (206) 684-4075.

Anyone up for *Pétanque?*

Eastlake *Bouledrome*

Fairview Avenue East, along the east shores of Lake Union, is currently undergoing a civic version of cosmetic surgery. In addition to the many new houseboats and road projects, the city and some of its private partners have been installing little community treasures here and there in the form of miniature parks. Seattle has an ordinance requiring vacant city land be used for public parks if not designated otherwise. The result: some of the weirdest parks in some of the oddest shapes and sizes.

You won't find one of these just anywhere—well, not outside France, anyway.

★ ★

This particular minipark is unique, but not for its size or shape; small as parks go, it's boringly rectangular. However, if you've ever had a hankering to get in a game of *pétanque* with your pals but couldn't find a *bouledrome* (pétanque court), I've got the perfect place for you. Along the Lake Union shoreline, with a sweet view of the lake and Queen Anne Hill, you'll find an official bouledrome where you and your buddies can come together for an action-packed game of pétanque.

Pétanque is a game invented in the south of France in 1907. It's similar to boccie or lawn bowling. It can be played solo, one on one, in doublets, or in triplets. The winner of a coin toss starts the game by carving a small circle in the dirt. Standing within the circle, the player first tosses a smaller wooden ball known as a "jack" toward the far end of the bouledrome. Players then try to roll their larger metal balls as close to the jack as possible. Other players attempt the same, while also trying to knock away other players' balls.

The Fairview Avenue East Bouledrome is a long, narrow, rectangular lane surrounded by a raised stone border with an opening at the far end. At the head of the course is a metal stanchion upon which is mounted a bronze plaque with the rules of the game engraved on its surface. Attached is also a mechanism for keeping score and a rake for grooming the gritty hardpan surface.

Oh, and don't forget to bring your own boules.

The Eastlake Bouledrome is located on the 2300 block of Fairview Avenue East just south of the Chinook Lake Union Moorage.

Go Play on the Freeway—or under It
I-5 Colonnade Park

This is one of the coolest parks in Seattle. No, I'm not just saying that. In a city like Seattle, known for its moisture from the sky, dry places to play outside year-round can't be taken lightly. As of December 2005, Seattle has been blessed with I-5 Colonnade Park, so named because of its dominant features—massive pillars pushing the freeway skyward.

The Pampered Palm

There are some curiosities that make you go "Wow!", some that cause you to burst into laughter, and others that might make you wince. However, every once in a while you find a curiosity that makes your face fold in on itself with confusion, leaving you wondering, *What the . . . ?*

My face contorted this way the first time I saw what appeared to be a lone palm tree growing out of the dry earth smack in the middle of Seattle's I-5 Colonnade Park. The park is tucked beneath I-5 along Lakeview Boulevard East, where massive colonnades support the freeway between the west slope of Capitol Hill and Lake Union.

On closer inspection, there are actually four trees planted within inches of one another on a tiny patch of earth. The planting is a part of Seattle's 1% for the Arts Program, which allocates that 1 percent of the capital construction cost of public projects be used to purchase and install works of art.

The artwork by Oakland, California, artist John Roloff is named *The Seventh Climate (Paradise Reconsidered).* The living artwork consists of the previously mentioned palm tree, as well as a magnolia tree, a birch tree, and a gum tree. These foreign trees represent diverse locations from Earth's northern and southern hemispheres. The

A palm tree grows beneath I-5, cared for by its own computer-controlled irrigation and illumination systems. If only we were all treated so well.

(continued)

under-the-freeway climate is actually computer controlled to create a climate approximating pre-freeway 1960 Seattle, including precipitation, sunlight, and moonlight. A premature baby in the neonatal unit of Seattle's Children's Hospital couldn't get better care.

I discovered the pampered palm and his pals when a mysterious rainbow caught my eye one dry, dusty, sun-drenched day. The rainbow arced across a space between the underside of the freeway and the park's hard-packed soil. The faux-weather is provided by a sprinkler system and a series of high-intensity lights, which supply the trees with moisture, light, and warmth.

The pampered palm is located in I-5 Colonnade Park. Visit the artist's Web site at www.johnroloff.com.

Located beneath the concrete lanes of I-5, the park is the only one of its kind in the country. It boasts some unique amenities: an off-leash dog run; 1% for the Arts' pampered palm tree (with its own lighting and irrigation system); and the park's most distinctive feature, an intricate mountain bike trail.

Rain or shine, bikers maneuver over the narrow, rocky, and virtually always-dry course, complete with all manner of obstacles and challenges. The public-private partnership to create the trail impressed me most. Every weekend volunteers grunted and groaned, pushing heavy wheelbarrow loads of rocks to build the course.

I-5 Colonnade Park runs along Lake View Boulevard East, south from where the road crosses under I-5, and is bounded by Boylston Avenue East on the west. For more information call Seattle Parks and Recreation at (206) 684-4075.

Here Come the Judge

Madison Park

After working for fifteen years on a beat that includes the Seattle neighborhood of Madison Park, I thought I knew a lot about the place. Turns out I knew very little. One of the more curious things I learned about a neighborhood I've been roaming for my entire career is that the *Seattle Star* (the *Seattle Times* predecessor) described Madison Park at the turn of the twentieth century as "Perhaps the only feudal state in the U.S."

Judge John J. McGilvra was a U.S. attorney for Washington Territory appointed by President Abraham Lincoln. Straying from politics, and obviously having an eye for real estate development, McGilvra established what could only be described as a 320-acre de facto fiefdom in what is now Madison Park.

Obviously being a man who believed a straight line was the quickest way between two points, both figuratively and literally, McGilvra snubbed his compass and built a road from downtown Seattle at Elliot Bay to Lake Washington, naming the street for our fourth President, James Madison. Madison Street runs west to east to 22nd Avenue East, where it hooks a left and continues northeast down Capitol Hill through Madison Valley to the lake. Future streets surrounding Madison would be platted on a more traditional north–south, east–west grid.

Rather than keeping the land for his personal use, or parceling it off and selling it to folks to build homes, the judge limited construction to cottages and charged folks a yearly tithe for the privilege of using the cottages. In the 1920s the judge finally surrendered his grip on the property and made the lots available for purchase.

Around this time McGilvra and Associates built a trolley line from Downtown to Madison Park and set aside twenty-one acres on the water for a park. If you think "tent city" has dubious connotations today, it wasn't so early on. On the portion of the shoreline south of Blaine Street, McGilvra built wooden platforms near the lake and

★ ★

allowed folks to pitch tents and, if they brought enough supplies in a wagon, spend the entire summer.

An interesting note: The final portion of East Madison Street beyond 43rd Avenue East isn't officially a part of the street. City records show that it's designated for park use as Waterway #4, from when it had been used as a landing for a ferryboat to and from Kirkland. Discussion is ongoing as to the final use of this "ghost" street.

Madison Park is located at Lake Washington in East Seattle. For more information visit http://madisonparkseattle.com.

Put It in the Ground, It'll Come Up Green

Washington Park Arboretum

I'm not overstating it when I say the Washington Park Arboretum, established in 1934 as a joint venture between the City of Seattle and the University of Washington, is a wondrous place to explore. Even on its busiest days you can still stake out your piece of forest solitude within its 230 sprawling acres of amazing flora of every description.

Our niece and nephew recently visited Seattle for the first time. He is a landscape professional back in Atlanta, although he's originally from New England. He made a comment that struck me as to just how fortunate we are to live in Seattle and to have such a magnificent place to visit. He said that as he looked around at the various Seattle landscapes, he identified several plant species that could grow in New England but not in Georgia and plants that he could find growing in Atlanta that wouldn't grow in New England, all happily flourishing together in Seattle.

This plant diversity is part of the arboretum's magic. Another portion of the recipe for success is in the way the park is laid out. Ringed by narrow roads and veined with gravel paths and soft grassy boulevards, whether you're driving or out for a casual stroll on a warm sunny day, the arboretum offers a lush abundance of plant species.

Among the natural growth, the park is divided into areas dedicated to specific species: oaks, Japanese maples, camellias, hollies, and giant sequoias. A stone pagoda sits at the crest of a hill in the heart of the park.

The south entrance of the Washington Park Arboretum is located at Lake Washington Boulevard and East Madison Street. The north entrance is at Lake Washington Boulevard and East Calhoun Street. For more information call (206) 543-8800 or visit http://depts.washington.edu/wpa/index.htm.

Hello, Carol!

I can't believe I've lived in Seattle for so long and I never knew that such a famous Broadway and Hollywood singer/actress as Carol Channing was born in the Emerald City on January 31, 1921, although she only lived in Seattle for two weeks before moving to San Francisco.

The Tony Award–winning entertainer is most famous for her roles in two musical plays: *Gentlemen Prefer Blondes* and *Hello, Dolly!*, in which she played the irrepressible title character. She had to be disappointed when the film versions of these plays came along and she was passed over for, respectively, Marilyn Monroe and Barbra Streisand.

Urban Wetland Adventure
Foster and Marsh Islands

Foster Island was homesteaded by John McGilvra in 1855. This was the same year that Thomas Mercer named Lake Union, in order to promote his vision of a ship canal uniting Lake Washington with Puget Sound.

The locks officially opened on July 4, 1917. The size of Foster Island increased when the locks were built, and the fill from the Montlake

Cut was added to the Foster Island shoreline. Also in 1917, the City of Seattle purchased Foster Island for $15,000. In 1936 the final version of the Olmsted Plan arrived, and Olmsted identified Foster Island as a site for an alpine garden! (Frederick Leissler, the de facto Washington Park Arboretum director, moved the alpine garden behind the Lodge House.)

Of course the history of Foster and Marsh Island far predates the arrival of folks like McGilvra and Mercer. In fact, people had been using the islands for thousands of years. It's said that local tribes used the island as a burial ground. Interestingly, by local custom, the deceased were placed suspended among the branches of low-growing trees and shrubs.

The wonderful waterfront trail that connects Marsh and Foster Islands was built with mitigation money from the arboretum's loss of sixty acres to the Evergreen Point Floating Bridge in 1961.

BOO!
Ghost Ramps

Arriving in Seattle, I was puzzled by the sight of incomplete ramps fraying off the freeway where Interstate 90 merges with I-5. It looked as though someone had chopped them off with a giant concrete cleaver, leaving them ghost ramps.

When we first moved to Seattle, we lived near the ghost ramps on Beacon Hill. One of our favorite activities was foraging beneath these ramps for the infamous flora that serve both as Seattle's official noxious weed and the city fruit. The I-90 ramps to nowhere—one set of two in the city—now go somewhere.

The ramps were surreal, and few seemed to have an answer as to why they hadn't completed their purpose—a civil engineer's joke, perhaps. Still, they were interesting to contemplate before they finally married I-90 to I-5. However, don't worry if you missed them, because there's another set of ghost ramps in this city.

Where the Washington Park Arboretum kisses the Montlake neighborhood, near where Route 520 spills onto I-5, similar ramps splay off

Ghost ramps are freeway ramps to nowhere. When someone asks where you're going and you say nowhere, you've got an entrance to get there.

the freeway. The ramps were intended to improve traffic flow through the arboretum.

I'm torn on this one. I love the arboretum, which is a treasure trove of flora and fauna and a venue for a variety of human activities. However, I don't love the traffic jamming the serpentine park road, which is in no way sufficient to handle the volume of traffic.

Again, surreal pops into my mind when I see these engineering anomalies as I stand beneath the ramps and try to imagine their intended destination. One ramp hangs high above where tons of soil was dumped during the Denny Regrade. In fact, collectors (especially of blue glass) still come to this location to hunt for treasure (which, by the by, is illegal). Another ramp bows down, headed in the opposite direction, seemingly begging to either be completed or put out of its misery.

★ ★

One of the ramps is often used by kids as a high dive into the lake on summer days. And although I've never actually seen anyone climbing on them, there are rock-climbing holds attached to one of the colonnades. And no, I've never been tempted to summit the ramps to nowhere. Okay, yes I have; fortunately, sanity has held sway—so far anyway.

The ghost ramps are located at Lake Washington Boulevard East and East Miller Street.

Seattle, Now and Zen

Japanese Garden (aka the Japanese Tea Garden)

I've tried to find the humor in many of these entries; however, this place, while not being particularly humorous, does leave one in a very good humor after a visit. The Japanese Garden, located near the south entrance of the Washington Park Arboretum at Lake Washington Boulevard East and East Madison Street, is well worth the trip.

On a recent visit I spoke with the garden's very knowledgeable top caretaker, Kathleen Blanchard. I asked Kathleen what she felt was the single most interesting aspect of the garden. I was certain she'd name a specific feature, like one of a number of marvelous statues or meticulously clipped plants. Nope. She said the most interesting aspect of the garden is the garden itself.

Kathleen said that while this garden may not be the oldest Japanese garden in America (that's in San Francisco), she believes it's the most authentic. In America we divide gardens into categories: Japanese, English, Zen, etc. Kathleen says that gardens in Japan are divided into time-period traditions. She said San Francisco's Japanese garden is quite beautiful; however, it's more eclectic in design, having plants and other features from Chinese and other non-Japanese traditions as well as items from a mixture of Japanese time periods.

As I strolled along the crushed-gravel paths, I was struck by the serenity. If you're wondering why I'd be struck by something one would expect to experience in a Japanese garden, it's because of the garden's location. A heavily traveled roadway runs within feet of the garden along its eastern boundary, and there's a busy parking lot and playfield to the south.

The Japanese Garden is located in the Washington Park Arboretum at 1075 Lake Washington Boulevard East. For more information call (206) 684-4725.

Seattle's Crusty Curmudgeon

Every town has its curmudgeons, and Emmet Watson was one of Seattle's best known. Watson was born in 1918. An orphan, he went on to paint a colorful portrait of himself in Seattle history. A rabid baseball fan, the eventual writer briefly played pro ball for the Seattle Rainiers after high school before earning a degree in communications from the University of Washington.

After a brief stint as a longshoreman, Watson spent the next fifty years as a journalist for the now defunct *Seattle Star,* the *Seattle PI,* and the *Seattle Times.* He also wrote four books over the course of his career. Watson was known for the humor he often injected into his progressive, sometimes bitingly sarcastic columns.

Watson's career took a giant leap forward when he scooped major national media with the revelation that Ernest Hemingway had not shot himself by accident in Ketchum, Idaho, as had been reported, but had committed suicide.

Watson was also known for his creation of Lesser Seattle, an effort to deter people from moving to his beloved Seattle during a period of heavy migration, particularly by people from California. Watson died on May 11, 2001, from issues stemming from surgery.

★ ★

A Roman Aqueduct?

Wilcox Bridge

As with most of the entries in this book, I have personal stories attached to this curiosity. The first thing to take in about this feature is its simple beauty. Built of brick and concrete in the style of the old Roman aqueducts, the Wilcox Bridge served a dual purpose. It was built in 1911 as a footbridge to make it easier for pedestrians to cross the, then, Valley Parkway. It also beautifully cloaked the water pipe that passes over the roadway.

This footbridge within the Washington Park Arboretum beautifully conceals an aqueduct within its brick facade.

Now for the personal aspect: There is only one thing about the bridge that surpasses its historic nature and pragmatic function. Perhaps if I give you a specific attribute, you'll get an idea of where I'm going with this. This bridge, as I said, is in the shape of a Roman arch, a muscular engineering structure. However, the bridge's clearance above the roadway is only 9 feet, 6 inches.

I'd like to tell you how many vehicles whose heights exceed 9-6 have attempted to fit their square truck through this round hole, but I lost count long ago. Coming from the south on Lake Washington Boulevard, large trucks trigger an overheight warning light and are able to bail at Boyer Avenue East. Hopefully the driver is paying attention. I think rather than flashing lights, the city might consider a device that reaches into the truck's cab and smacks the driver on the back of the head.

Approaching from the north, there are no fewer than five warning signs. Still, overheight trucks—the lucky ones—continue to screech to a halt before slamming into the bridge, and then muck up traffic as they attempt to maneuver out. Some drivers continue to challenge physics.

I once responded to a rental company truck whose driver passed under the bridge in extraordinary fashion. Rather than becoming stuck, or stopping on initial impact, this truck slammed through and continued for several hundred yards, its container having been ripped open like a sardine can, spewing items of furniture all over the roadway.

And what did he say when I questioned him about the "accident"? "I thought I could make it!"

Wilcox Bridge is located south of where Lake Washington Boulevard East and East Foster Island Road intersect.

Boat, Sweet Home
Lake Union

In a city known for water that falls from the sky, it's only natural that people would have figured out how to utilize this resource in every possible way. It's not enough for some folks that water inundates, inculcates, and saturates much of Seattle life—apparently some people need to get even a tad cozier with the wet stuff. How cozy? Seattle boasts more people living aboard houseboats than any other city in America. There are around 500 houseboats in the city, and I can tell

★ ★

Home, home, on the water—where the salmon and
the jet-skiers play.

you that there's no sign this lifestyle is about to go out of fashion, so
landlubbers beware.

My police beat includes many houseboats along the shores of Lake
Union. I've watched as ever-increasing docks and houseboats are built
each year. And believe me when I tell you these folks are not losing
anything by way of amenities living on the waves. Some of these floating homes, especially the new construction, are among the most beautiful homes in Seattle. Who wouldn't be happy with no lawn to mow?
Well, I suppose those who aren't could always manicure the milfoil?

If you want to take a peek at these floating flats, I'd suggest viewing them by boat. If you need to do it by land, consider an urban
hike—much of the road is very narrow, and by narrow I mean not a
pleasure to drive. In fact, it's a lot like playing a video game where
you dodge cars and pedestrians; only you have no missiles or lasers to
eliminate these hazards.

To get there from Downtown, head north on Westlake Avenue to the south end of Lake Union and bear right to Fairview Avenue North. Drive north past a row of marinas and great restaurants. When you get to the fork in the road, bear left and continue on Fairview Avenue North to miles of floating neighborhoods.

The houseboats are docked in the Lake Union Eastlake neighborhood.

Trivia

Seattle's houseboat population is the largest in the United States and the largest in the world east of the Orient.

A Bridge to Somewhere

Evergreen Point Floating Bridge

Where is the longest floating bridge in the world? Time's up: Seattle. Known locally as the 520 Floating Bridge or the Evergreen Point Floating Bridge, officially it's the Governor Albert D. Rossellini Floating Bridge. If Seattle had only one floating bridge, folks could simply call it the Floating Bridge, but Seattle has three. The second- and fifth-longest floating bridges on Earth are located a few miles south.

Why a floating bridge? The Vashon Glacier gouged Lake Washington exceptionally deep, fjord deep. During the last ice age, the glacial gods trenched the lake between what is now Seattle and its eastside suburbs as they retreated north. The lake's extreme depth and muddy bottom made more classical bridge designs impractical. Seattle's relationship with water is infamous, so it's only natural that in 1960 folks would build a bridge that floats. The first car christened it on August 28, 1963.

★ ★

This floating bridge is built like a ship, separated into several water-tight compartments, or sections, across the length of the span, and is tethered with a series of anchors. The east and west "high rises" allow vessels north and south access. For large vessels and in severe weather, the center span opens to allow passage and relieve pressure.

The bridge is also unique for a political reason. When the bridge opened, tollbooths were operated to pay for its construction. Once users paid for the bridge, however, the tollbooths were eliminated and now serve as bus stops. Plans are being considered to replace the aging structure—and the tollbooths.

I've marveled at the bridge's ability to split the lake into two separate realities. On a breezy day, water on one side of the bridge can be as choppy as a crowded kiddie pool, while the opposite side is glass smooth. I'm not sure why this fascinates me; it's simple physics. I guess for me it's just one of those "shiny" objects in life that steals my attention and leaves me gazing like a contented dolt.

The Governor Albert D. Rossellini Floating Bridge is located on Portage Bay in the Montlake neighborhood, crossing Lake Washington toward the Bellevue-Kirkland area.

4

Southwest

Seattle's southwest encompasses *the city west of the Duwamish River, location of Seattle's original non-Indian settlement. It includes the city's highest elevation at 520 feet above sea level. The largest slice, and the city's biggest neighborhood, West Seattle, is a place with great parks, quaint neighborhoods, and sandy beaches. The most well-known neighborhood is Seattle's first, Alki, which reminds me of a story. New to Seattle, a friend and I were Downtown waiting for a bus when we noticed alki on a bus destination sign. My buddy, not a stranger to an alcoholic beverage or two, mispronounced the sign as "Al-Kee."*

My friend said, "Al-Kee? That's where I want to go!"

A Seattleite, less than impressed with the new arrival's commentary, corrected him with a haughtily dismissive expression and an overly enunciated "Alk-Eye."

If you've seen a spectacular photograph of the Seattle skyline, day or night, chances are it was taken from West Seattle. West Seattle is mélange of working-class neighborhoods, artist enclaves, and homes possessing stunning views of the Puget Sound and the Olympic and Cascade Mountains.

If you haven't been to West Seattle on a hot sunny day, get there. Alki Beach is the closest thing Seattle has to a California-type beach.

Seattle's Coney Island
Luna Park

The fun lasted only about half a decade, but for that time (1907–1913) Luna Park, often referred to as the Coney Island of the West, provided an amazing array of entertainment for communities surrounding Elliot Bay, which forces one to ask why we're not still riding the roller coaster today?

A short ferry ride from Seattle, the West Seattle attraction, built on piers above the headwaters of the Duwamish River, where the original Seattle pioneers landed, was a popular destination until its premature

A Taste of Old Seattle

Luna Park evokes thoughts of the Coney Island–style amusement park whose lights once sparkled across Elliott Bay from West Seattle. Well, the park may be long gone, but fortunately you can still enjoy a bit of this little-known piece of West Seattle history.

Since March 18, 1989, the Luna Park Cafe has encapsulated a piece of the Luna Park experience while serving up traditional American fare, including huge burgers, old-fashioned milk shakes, and, a nod to the modern, some fine Northwest microbrews.

The cafe gives you a two-fer, because it's like eating in a museum surrounded by colorful memorabilia, including many early-era Seattle storefront signs. From early spring to late fall, you can eat alfresco on the patio.

To complete the Luna Amusement Park experience, the Luna Cafe has an honest-to-goodness ride: a Batmobile! Just remember to bring a pocketful of quarters—not just for the Dark Knight's diminutive demise. The only evidence left of the park's original location can be seen about once a decade, when extremely low tides reveal remnants of those piers jutting up from the muck. One can almost hear the whoops, hollers, and screams of folks as they careened around the track on the figure-eight roller coaster, cascaded down the water slide, or braved the Cave of Mystery.

Its own city at the time, West Seattle wanted to have "the greatest amusement park in the Northwest." In fact, one park attraction may have achieved the equivalent title of "the greatest bar in the Northwest"—reputedly home to the best-stocked bar on Elliott Bay.

wheels but also for the 1958 jukebox. For your convenience, they've installed mini-jukeboxes in the booths. Got a few quarters left? Feed Pepé the Dancing Clown, or impress your friends with a temporary tattoo.

Luna Park Cafe is located at 2918 Southwest Avalon Way. For more information call (206) 935-7250 or visit www.lunapark cafe.com.

Talk about nostalgia. No, really; come here and talk about the nostalgia that surrounds you as you munch on some of the tastiest munchies in West Seattle.

★ ★

Unfortunately, this created some unintended consequences. Many West Seattleites, upset that their city council would do nothing about the bar, which attracted hordes of barflies from Seattle, petitioned Seattle for annexation. The vote went 325–8 for annexation, and the short-lived city of West Seattle was no more.

Why isn't Luna Park still busy amusing us today? A "battle of morals" had broken out, pitting those for the park against those opposing it. After war erupted between the pro-Luna party forces and the forces of the party-poopers, the poopers caught the partiers in a scandal that city officials would be hard-pressed to equal in modern times. Seems the manager of Luna Park was a partner in the Seattle police chief's business enterprise: a 500-room brothel.

The scandal proved too much for the partiers to defend, and the party-poopers pooped on the Luna Park party, assuring the big bar's demise and, along with it, the amusement park. Assets were trashed or sold off in 1913. The last remaining portion, the swimming facility, called the natatorium, hung on until 1931, when it burned to the ground.

Going Wild in the City, but Not Like You Think
Camp Long

Okay, so say you're in your Seattle home seated around the dinner table. You're chatting with your family—hubby, wifey, or significant other-y, the kids, and your Cockapoo named Spoodle. The topic of summer camping comes up.

"Let's rent a cabin some place where we can go hiking and maybe get some rock climbing lessons," you say to a round of applause and three yips from Spoodle. You pull out a dog-eared (sorry, Spoodle) copy of *The Big Book of Outdoor Stuff to Do,* flip it open. Casting caution to the wind, you cover your eyes and, with an eager index finger spiraling down, let serendipity find your destination. You snatch up your magnifying glass and read the tiny print under your finger: the Middle of Nowhere, and MapQuest says it'll take you seventeen hours, fifty-three and a half minutes on rugged, rutted, and rooted primitive roads to get there.

Still excited about your camping trip? No? Then have I got the place for you—and get this, you won't even have to leave Seattle. Camp Long is a wilderness adventure awaiting you smack in the middle of an urban jungle. If you check out Camp Long on Seattle Parks and Recreation's Web site, the first thing they tell you is, "Camp Long is one of Seattle's best kept secrets." I suppose inclusion in this book doesn't help if they want to maintain that claim, but I'm not about to apologize for it—this place is cool.

Camp Long's sixty-eight acres of dense forest is located adjacent to the east side of the West Seattle Golf Course. You can rent one of the cabins for overnight camping, take rock-climbing lessons, or hike through the forest, where you'll encounter wildlife and may even be treated to the sight of an elusive barred owl family that's occasionally seen in the park.

I'm not kidding about this place; you've got to see it for yourself. You won't believe what you've been missing. So next time you crave the scent of fir, spruce, and pine, especially if you're pressed for time, reserve some quality time with Mother Nature and book some cabin time in one of the ten lodges nestled within Seattle's city limits.

Camp Long is located at 5200 35th Avenue Southwest. For more information call (206) 684-7434 or visit www.seattle.gov/parks/Environment/camplong.htm.

Seattle Has One, Too
Statue of Liberty

I remember that when I first saw it many years ago, I'd been totally unaware of its existence. A 7½-foot-tall "mini-me" of the Statue of Liberty stands sentinel on Alki Beach. It took me by surprise. Being from the East Coast and having climbed up to the crown of the original, I wasn't sure how I felt about it—I mean, part of the impact of Lady Liberty in New York Harbor is her sheer size.

★ ★

Renovated in recent years, Seattle's diminutive Lady Liberty is a nod to her East Coast cousin and to Seattle's first pioneer colony, which they called New York–Alki.

However, Seattle's diminutive Lady Liberty grew on me and I became fond of her in short order. The Boy Scouts of America had given her to the city as a gift in 1952. Her importance became clearer to me after the attacks of 9/11, when she became the natural focal and rallying point for Seattleites who wished to express their solidarity with their fellow Americans suffering in New York City.

In July 2006 the statue was taken down for much-needed repairs. Weather and vandalism had taken their toll on the old girl over the

★ ★

past half-century. The spruced-up Little Lady Liberty reassumed her rightful place on Alki Beach, quite appropriately raising her torch high for all to see during a rededication ceremony on September 11, 2007.

The city has built a beautiful plaza befitting the miniature statue of such major stature. The plaza features stone-paved walkways that flow between lively gardens, surrounding the effigy. For those who visit her at night, lights have been added to enhance the experience, bathing her features in a soft golden glow.

Seattle's Statue of Liberty is located at Alki Beach, 61st Avenue Southwest.

Surf's Up
Alki

As I mentioned earlier, my first memory of Alki involves an improper pronunciation of the word. A friend of mine and I were Downtown waiting for a bus. A destination displayed above a coach's windshield read ALKI. My buddy, not a stranger to intoxicating beverages, perked up and declared, "Al-Kee! I want to go there!" "Alki" is actually Chinook jargon (a mixture of English, French, and Chinook words) meaning "by and by."

"Getting it," I laughed and nodded vigorously. As you know, a well-intended, and apparently well-offended, Seattleite set us straight with our first lesson in "Seattleese." "Alk-Eye," she pronounced with overly affected diction.

Alki is a neighborhood in West Seattle surrounding, and including, Alki Point at the southernmost point of Elliot Bay. Alki is where the Denny Party planted the seeds for what would become the city of Seattle. The original name of the 6-block, eight-lot settlement was New York Alki. Pioneer leader Arthur Denny soon relocated the settlement to what is known today as Pioneer Square.

A few folks held on at Alki before eventually joining the others. Charles Terry traded land to Doc Maynard for land in Pioneer Square. Maynard eventually sold his Alki holdings to Hans Hanson and Knud

Olson, who, with a simple lantern on a post, gave birth to the Alki Lighthouse.

The oldest house in Alki, the Bernard family home, built in 1904, is currently the well-reviewed Alki Homestead Restaurant. More evidence of the independent spirit of old-time Alki folks can be seen where the modest house of a homeowner who refused to skedaddle remains awkwardly tucked between two high-rise condominium buildings.

Alki, whose summer beach concert tradition stretches back to the early 1900s, hosts the Seattle Music Fest every August. While at Alki Point, take a look at the monument commemorating the Denny Party. It lists the names of the original pioneers who landed at Alki in 1851.

Last, but far from least, there is no place better in Seattle to view, sketch, paint, or photograph the Seattle skyline.

Alki is located in southwest Seattle, roughly Alki Avenue SW at Southwest Admiral Way (if the streets met).

5

South

Although having its *fair share of neighborhoods from working class to affluent, the south end of Seattle is best described as the industrial heart of the city. There's King County International Airport (Boeing Field), which is also home to some Boeing Company activities and many supporting businesses. At the far southwest end is the impressive Museum of Flight, where, incidentally, my former police partner was married.*

You may chuckle at the name of one industrial area of the south end, as I do for the images it creates in my juvenile mind: South Park. Need I say more? South Seattle is a crisscross of railways, warehouses, and light to heavy industrial enterprises, with a smattering of neighborhoods and large and small retail stores and restaurants.

The southeast section is dense neighborhoods mixed with apartment complexes, middle-class family homes, and business districts. As you move toward the shores of Lake Washington you'll find a park that gives visitors an idea of what all of Seattle once looked like before non-Indian settlers arrived. Here you'll find Seward Park, one of Seattle's oldest parks, which now, with portions closed to motor vehicles, offers some of the best hikes within the city.

You Knew There Had to Be One

Seattle Barista Academy

This comes under the heading: Where else but in Seattle would a Barista Academy exist? In fact, if asked as a question on a quiz show, I'd bet 100

★ ★

percent of the contestants would answer, "Seattle." In Seattle, coffee isn't just a commercial enterprise. It's also a science and, to an almost absurd degree (and I count myself among the absurd), an art.

What's unique about this particular institution of higher learning is that it's open to both those who desire to go pro and the latté layperson. If you've ever wondered about whether the passion for great java in Seattle was just a passing fad, the existence of such a school proves it.

Their motto could be "From Bean to Barista." The academy, rightly so, sees the barista as the next-to-last link in a chain stretching back to the coffee bean, forward to the barista, and finally to the last link, the consumer.

Whether you're a coffeeshop owner interested in improving your staff's skill level or you're serious about enhancing your own already spectacular skills to the realm of the extraordinary, the academy offers some excellent perks. They'll pick you up at SeaTac Airport, take you to the hotel, and then bring you from your hotel to class each day.

Have a staff in need of a little barista tutoring, but you don't have the means to send staff to Seattle? The Seattle Barista Academy (SBA) will send a superstar barista to you. That's right; a nationally ranked barista competitor (according to the SBA Web site) will teach a course personalized especially for your business.

And who's responsible for this caffeine craziness? We'll put it squarely on the shoulders of Bob Burgess. While Howard Schultz may be the specialty coffee store king, Burgess could rightly be called the espresso drink and coffee cart king—which, by the way, is much more alliterative.

Seattle's coffee pioneer and innovator extraordinaire, Burgess has been importing espresso machines and manufacturing coffee carts since the mid-1980s. Burgess opened the doors to the Seattle Barista Academy in 2003, and from what I can see, Seattleites still love their coffee—art, science, or otherwise.

The Seattle Barista Academy is located at 1000 Southwest 34th Street, Building W-2, Suite A, Renton. For more information call (800) 927-3286 or visit www.seattlebaristaacademy.com.

A Tropical Paradise It's Not

Harbor Island

When most people think of islands, they think Aruba, Jamaica, or Maui. (I'm always thinking of Maui.) They think sandy beaches, palm trees, sea-foam teal water, and mai tais. A Pacific Northwesterner might consider Washington's beautiful San Juan Islands, with their misty, Douglas fir–dotted landscapes.

When we consider man-made structures, normally we think of buildings, roads, and bridges. But do you ever think of a man-made island? Where the Duwamish River flows into Elliot Bay, in view of Downtown, sits Harbor Island, a 406-acre man-made industrial atoll.

When workers built Harbor Island in 1909 using millions of tons of excavated earth from the Denny Regrade and dredged from the Duwamish, it was the world's largest man-made island. It's still America's biggest. The multiuse island, which boasts a permanent population of three people, is home to a variety of businesses, including petroleum storage, container shipping, shipbuilding, warehousing, metal fabricating, and a publishing house.

Now if you're thinking of lounging on Harbor Island, instead of soft white sand you'll be digging your toes into gravel. Instead of swaying palms, you'll have to settle for the shade of acres of giant shipping containers. However, finding shade is not normally a difficult endeavor in Seattle—it's the sun we're more interested in finding. And as for the water, no azure waves lap at this island. The only thing I can guarantee about this water is that it's wet, dark, and very—very—cold.

While not exactly my idea of a sailing, tanning, or surfing vacation paradise, Harbor Island provides functional land for large-scale industrial and other enterprises, which allows land on shore to be available for other uses.

Now I don't want to dissuade you from packing up the cooler and a picnic basket, scooping up the kiddies, and heading on down to Harbor Island on the next sunny day, but I would caution you that you'll probably have a hard time driving that beach umbrella into the creosote-soaked piers.

★ ★

Harbor Island is located in Elliott Bay off 16 Avenue SW and South-west Spokane Street.

Flights of Fancy
The Museum of Flight

Set on twelve acres at the south end of the King County Airport, the Museum of Flight (MOF) offers both indoor and outdoor exhibits that will capture your imagination. The museum offers over 150 "histori-cally significant" air-and spacecraft and the West Coast's largest avia-tion and space library and archives.

So, what does the MOF consider historically significant? Well, there's the only supersonic jetliner, a British Airways Concorde, on display on the West Coast; the first jet Air Force One; a prototype for the Boeing 747; an Apollo Command Module; and a Soviet Sputnik spacecraft. You can also view Boeing's original 1909 two-story red-barn manufacturing facility, the oldest aircraft plant in existence in the United States.

The museum's Great Gallery is jaw dropping. At six stories, the three-million-cubic-foot, steel-framed-glass exhibit hall houses forty-one full-size aircraft. Twenty-two of them, including a Douglas DC-3 weighing nine tons, hang from the ceiling as if time stopped while they were in midflight.

You want a hands-on experience? Try out the virtual-reality simu-lators, or clamber into the cockpit of an F-18 Hornet or an SR-71 Blackbird. And please don't forget to stroll through the Personal Cour-age Wing, which pays tribute to the brave aviators who fought in the danger-filled skies of World War II.

I also have a personal story to go with this museum. On September 1, 2001, I was honored to be in the wedding party of my patrol part-ner, Mark. The wedding and reception took place inside the Museum of Flight. Not exactly traditional, we even took the wedding photos within the fuselage of an old Boeing jetliner.

During the event, we witnessed our own "historic flight." During the traditional bouquet toss, Tania, the beautiful bride, launched the flower bundle into the air. The flowers rocketed so high the bouquet actually snagged on a fire sprinkler head and dangled there. A gaggle of single women stared in suspended anticipation, eyes riveted sky-ward, until a facilities worker climbed a ladder and sent the bouquet plummeting back into the wedding's atmosphere—the bridesmaids on the blooms like sharks on chum.

The Museum of Flight is located at 9404 East Marginal Way South. The museum is open daily except Thanksgiving and Christmas. Admission is free the first Thursday of the month from 5:00 to 9:00 p.m., thanks to Wells Fargo. Parking is free. For more information call (206) 764-5720 or visit www.museumofflight.org.

How It Was Back When

Seward Park

"Out in the boonies." Seward Park, a beautiful peninsula park jutting out into Lake Washington in south Seattle, almost didn't happen because it was considered "too far out of town." Fortunately folks with foresight thought differently, and the city bought the land in 1911 for $322,000.

For me the natural history of the park exceeds its human history. Thirteen thousand years ago a 4,000-foot glacier left this little peninsula of bedrock exposed after gouging out Lake Washington. There's some interesting natural history beneath the waves between the park and Mercer Island to the east. About 1,100 years ago a large chunk of Mercer Island forest fell into the lake. Remarkably, the trees remained upright. However, folks couldn't see the forest for the water.

When the lake level was lowered 9 feet after engineers opened the ship canal and locks in Ballard, it exposed the treetops. These trees were initially topped to mitigate the shipping hazard; 186 trees were also logged, harvested from the lake, and used for lumber. The lake's frigid temperatures had preserved the trees, which had been about 150 years old when they entered the lake.

★ ★

Fred Hutchinson

Many people are familiar with the world-renowned Fred Hutchinson Cancer Research Institute created by Fred's brother, Dr. William Hutchinson, and home to no fewer than three Nobel laureates. But how familiar are folks with its namesake?

Fred Hutchinson, known by fans as "Hutch," was born August 12, 1919, and was a true Seattle baseball legend, having enjoyed professional careers as both a player and a manager.

At age nineteen Hutch won twenty-five games for the AA Seattle Rainiers, earning him Minor League Player of the Year. After a brief stint with the Detroit Tigers, his career was interrupted by service in the U.S. Navy during World War II, where he attained the rank of lieutenant commander.

After the war Hutch rejoined the Tigers, where he went on to a stellar eleven-year career. He has the dubious distinction of being the pitcher to give up the longest home run in Ted Williams's career. That Fenway Park (Boston) seat, at 502 feet, is painted red to this day.

A promising managing career was cut short when Hutch was diagnosed with cancer. Fred Hutchinson died on November 12, 1964. He is a member of the Cincinnati Reds Hall of Fame, and in 1999 the *Seattle Post-Intelligencer* named him Seattle's Athlete of the 20th Century.

One negative result of lowering the lake level was that some old-growth Douglas fir trees died. When the trees were cut into, the rings showed that the area had suffered a significant forest fire right about the time Columbus hit the New World.

Named for President Lincoln's secretary of state, William Seward, Seward Park is a great place to walk or bike through the old-growth timber on the 2.4-mile trail. The trail was once open to cars, but the farthest section of the loop drive has been closed to motor vehicles.

My wife often took our children to Seward Park on sunny summer days to enjoy the beach—where once was water and marsh—thanks to the digging of a certain canal located many miles to the north.

Seward Park is located at 5898 Lake Washington Boulevard South. For more information call (206) 684-4396 or visit www.seattle.gov/parks/environment/seward.htm.

Baseball: Before the Ms

Sick's Stadium

Seattle has a rich minor league baseball history, which continues to this day—by extension—with the Tacoma Rainiers (AAA Mariners) and the Everett Aqua Sox (A Mariners), but some folks may not be aware that Major League Baseball attempted to take hold in Seattle before the 1977 arrival of the Seattle Mariners. The Seattle Pilots took a stab at planting the MLB's flag in the Jet City in 1969. Unfortunately, the lifespan of the expansion Pilots was extremely short-lived, lasting only one season.

The primary problem was the venue. Sick's Stadium, opened in 1938 and named for Emil Sick, owner of the Seattle Rainiers minor league baseball team and the Rainier Brewing Company, wasn't quite the home that major league ball club owners desired. In 1965 the Cleveland Indians considered a move to Seattle, which was seen as a potentially excellent major league baseball town, but the poor condition of Sick's made any deal impossible. The stadium was so sick that the team's single season ended in bankruptcy for the Pilots and resulted in the team's moving to Milwaukee in 1970.

Although crumbling at the end, there are some little known gems embedded in Sick's Stadium history from its heyday. For example, in 1946 it was home to the Seattle Steelheads of the West Coast Baseball

Association, Negro League. Sick's had been considered by many to be one of the nation's best minor league ballparks. The stadium also hosted a wide range of concerts, the pinnacle being Elvis Presley's performance in 1957. Incidentally, that concert was attended by Seattle's own Jimi Hendrix, who would one day play his own show at Sick's Stadium, as did his music-era colleague, Janis Joplin. The stadium was demolished in 1979. A plaque marks its former setting at the present-day Lowes Home Improvement location.

Sick's Stadium was located at 2700 Rainier Avenue South.

The End of the Line
Taejon Park

This two-acre patch of green on south Beacon Hill, which sits above the well-traveled lanes of Interstate 90, is a city park with some interesting, albeit disparate amenities. And I'm not talking about the black-asphalt terminus of the freeway that began in Boston and ends in Seattle or the I-90 bike trail, which skirts the western edge of Taejon Park.

The preeminent feature of this park is a Korean pagoda near the south end. The pagoda was built, and the park dedicated, in 1995 to honor Seattle's sister city of Taejon. Taejon, South Korea, is one of a sorority of Seattle sister cities scattered around the planet.

Taejon is Seattle's thirteenth sister city, named on October 4, 1989. Taejon, South Korea's sixth-largest city and a provincial capital, is located about 100 miles south of Seoul. In Korean *Taejon* means "great field." Seattle Mayor Charles Royer signed the official proclamation in Taejon as head of a delegation to that city.

For me the real treat was watching the craftsmen and artisans as they built the beautiful pagoda. I was so impressed with the finished work, even when only naked wood prior to painting, that I actually hoped they'd leave it bare. However, when I glimpsed the completed pagoda, intricately painted in such spectacular colors—all I can say is, it simply has to be experienced.

This intricately appointed pagoda marks the endpoint on I-90's 3,000-mile journey from Boston.

Stroll the bike path, or tread the grass north about a hundred yards or so, and you'll come to a plaque introducing you to the sculpture *Equality*. It's an interesting piece of art and a bit enigmatic. In fact, although I abhor graffiti, some young delinquent would-be artist added his own contribution to the piece when he scarred the upper portion of the sculpture with the words "I don't get it."

Perhaps he missed the plaque with the title and artist information. The piece was created by artists-designers Ken Leback and Rolon Bert Garner in 1995. I could go into my interpretation of the artwork, but then again, what the hell do you care what I think?

Taejon Park is located at 1144 Sturgus Avenue South. For more information call (206) 684-4075 or visit www.seattle.gov/parks/park_detail.asp?ID=4400.

★ ★

Because It's There

Jim Whittaker is an American legend. Born in Seattle on February 10, 1929, Whittaker was destined, along with his twin brother, Lou, to pursue adventures around the world. Whittaker began climbing at a young age and was a Mount Rainier guide by the time he was twenty-one years old.

On May 1, 1963, Jim Whittaker became the first American to summit Mount Everest. He and three other climbers reached the top despite having depleted their oxygen supply. Whittaker celebrated by planting an American flag.

Not satisfied with being the first American to summit the tallest mountain on Earth, he led the first American team to summit the second tallest, and perhaps even more difficult, K2.

Having become friendly with the Kennedys, in 1965 Whittaker led a team of climbers, including Robert F. Kennedy, up Mount Kennedy (13,095 feet) in the Yukon Territory, Canada, which had been recently named in honor of RFK's brother, the slain American president.

Whittaker, the first full-time employee of REI, now serves as chairman of the board of Magellan Navigation, a company that manufactures handheld global positioning system (GPS) devices. He released his autobiography, *A Life on the Edge: Memoirs of Everest and Beyond,* in 1999.

A Long Time Coming
Northwest African American Museum

The "official" idea for a Northwest African American Museum (NAAM) had been floating around since 1981. Finally, in 1993 the African

American Heritage and Cultural Center organized as a group, with a board of directors and the project overseen by the mayor's office. In 2003 the organization purchased the Colman School building, built in 1909, from the Seattle School District. That building had been considered almost since the idea for the museum was conceived.

The museum, which overlooks the I-90 lid, overcame a lack of funds and conflicting visions to come into existence as the premier institution of its kind in the Pacific Northwest. The museum honors and celebrates four aspects of African-American life: art, education, history, and culture.

At the time of this writing, the NAAM doesn't exhibit its own collection but those from other national, regional, and local resources. This keeps the exhibits continually fresh, new, and exciting. The museum isn't limited to the history of black Americans descended from the crime of slavery. This museum is as interested in the future as it is with the past. It also records the history being made every day by newly arriving black immigrants, currently primarily arriving from East African nations such as Somalia and Ethiopia.

The Northwest African American Museum is located at 2300 South Massachusetts Street. The museum is closed Monday and Tuesday. For more information visit http://naamnw.org/.

index

index

index

index

index

index

index

index

about the author

Steve Pomper lives in the Pacific Northwest. His first book, *Is There a Problem, Officer? A Cop's Inside Scoop on Avoiding Traffic Tickets*, was published by the Lyons Press in 2007. *It Happened in Seattle* (Globe Pequot Press) is scheduled for publication in 2009.

Steve operates an interactive Web site at www.stevepomper.com. He enjoys riding his Harley, hanging out with his three kids, and spending time with his firefighter wife of thirty years, Jody.